城市轨道交通客运服务英语口语

Spoken English for Urban Rail Transit Customer Service

主　　编　丁新宇
副 主 编　宫若潇　孙晨婷
参编人员　项柳青

"互联网+"教材

全书配套资源

北京理工大学出版社
BEIJING INSTITUTE OF TECHNOLOGY PRESS

版权专有 侵权必究

图书在版编目（CIP）数据

城市轨道交通客运服务英语口语 = Spoken English for Urban Rail Transit Customer Service / 丁新宇主编. —北京：北京理工大学出版社，2019.1（2021.12重印）
ISBN 978 - 7 - 5682 - 6546 - 1

Ⅰ.①城⋯　Ⅱ.①丁⋯　Ⅲ.①城市铁路 - 客运服务 - 英语 - 口语 - 高等学校 - 教材　Ⅳ.①U239.5

中国版本图书馆 CIP 数据核字（2018）第 287461 号

出版发行 / 北京理工大学出版社有限责任公司	
社　　址 / 北京市海淀区中关村南大街 5 号	
邮　　编 / 100081	
电　　话 /（010）68914775（总编室）	
（010）82562903（教材售后服务热线）	
（010）68948351（其他图书服务热线）	
网　　址 / http：// www.bitpress.com.cn	
经　　销 / 全国各地新华书店	
印　　刷 / 三河市天利华印刷装订有限公司	
开　　本 / 787 毫米 × 1092 毫米　1/16	
印　　张 / 9	责任编辑 / 梁铜华
字　　数 / 208 千字	文案编辑 / 梁铜华
版　　次 / 2019 年 1 月第 1 版　2021 年 12 月第 4 次印刷	责任校对 / 黄拾三
定　　价 / 28.00 元	责任印制 / 李　洋

图书出现印装质量问题，请拨打售后服务热线，本社负责调换

前言

随着城市化进程的加快,我国的城市轨道交通建设也进入了快速发展期,许多城市已经运行了轨道交通,还有些城市正在建设轨道交通。轨道交通已经成为大城市公共交通的主要工具,有效地解决了城市交通拥堵的问题。城市轨道交通的发展对轨道交通专业人才的要求也不断提高,英语能力是其中重要的方面。比如要求技术人员能用英语和国外公司进行技术交流、谈判与合作。此外很多到中国旅游或工作的外国人会选择地铁或轻轨等出行,这需要从业者熟练掌握轨道交通客运服务英语、车站英语等。

现有的教材中口语教材较少,多数教材偏重阅读,与相关的岗位培训要求有一定的距离。本书的编写主要是为了弥补这些不足,加强对从业人员的轨道交通客运服务英语、车站英语方面的口头交流的训练。

教材结构:

本教材主要由单元和附录组成。全书有5个单元,内容包括日常客运服务、票务服务、地铁安全、特殊情况下的客运服务、大型活动中的客运服务,每个单元下面有3~4课的内容,共有17课,内容包括:问询和指引,投诉和建议,广播,买票和检票,售票机故障,不同情况下的票务处理,安全检查,车站内的安全警示,站台上的安全警示,帮助病人、伤者和残疾人,失物招领,处理紧急情况,恶劣天气下的运行,问候和问询,首末班车,公共服务、亚运会等,这些都是学生在工作中遇到的场景,覆盖了客运服务的主要工作内容,具有实用性和专业性的特点。每个单元有明确的学习目标,每课主要涉及以下4个部分:导入(warming-up)、情景对话(situational dialogues)、练习(exercises)和自我评估(self-evaluation)。

1) 导入部分:包括图片与单词词组的匹配与学习或者是与主题相关问题的讨论,唤起学生对本单元学习内容的兴趣,并通过讨论、头脑风暴等对学生进行思维训练和口语表达能力的训练。

2) 情景对话:针对客运服务的各种情景编写情景对话,突出对话的实用性、职业性和专业性,营造口语学习气氛。对话后列出了单词词组表,并对对话中的难句、要句进行了总结、分析和延伸。

3) 练习部分:由选8~10个单词或词组填句子、填写1~2个对话并表演、3~4个不同情景的角色扮演以及4~5个句子的中译英4个练习组成。这些练习的目的主要是训练学生职业英语口语能力，同时帮助学生掌握专业词汇和短语以及重要句型的应用技巧。

4）自我评估：每篇课文都有自我评估，主要是督促学生在学习过程中加强对自己学习过程、学习成果的反思和总结，做到查漏补缺，提高他们的学习成效和自主学习能力。

本书的附录包括单词和短语、地铁广播、安全警示、杭州市主要旅游景点、体育项目名称、参考答案以及参考文献7个部分。

教材特点：

本教材在编写过程中，兼顾行业需求以及学生的学习需求，以培养学生的职业英语交流能力为目标。编写中遵循职业性、专业性和实用性的原则，内容丰富新颖、主题明确、覆盖面广。教材共编写了69个情景对话，涉及了客运服务的不同工作场景，内容突出了口语能力的训练和培养。本教材的特点如下：

1）突出口语能力培养，注重口语练习和模仿。
2）从真实的工作场景中选取素材，内容实用，富于实践性和职业性。
3）设计各种各样的工作任务，以任务驱动教学引导学生的学习。
4）图文并茂，便于学生直观理解内容，激发学生的学习兴趣。
5）练习形式多样，注重互动性、操作性和趣味性。

本书由杭州万向职业技术学院丁新宇担任主编，并负责总体设计、审稿等工作。杭州万向职业技术学院的宫若潇以及上海邦德职业技术学院的孙晨婷担任副主编。各章的具体分工如下：丁新宇编写了第二单元和第四单元以及附录1、附录2、附录6和附录7，宫若潇和孙晨婷编写了第一单元、第三单元以及第五单元，其中宫若潇负责编写了这些单元的部分课文中的一些对话、三个单元学习目标以及这三个单元共10篇课文中的导入、单词表、难句解释、练习和自我评估表，孙晨婷主要负责这些单元的课文对话编写。宫若潇还负责附录1、附录6的编写和本书的排版工作，孙晨婷编写了附录3、附录4和附录5。福州地铁的项柳青编写了教材中的中文对话及附录3、附录4和附录5的中文句子。杭州万向职业技术学院的律岚和蒋丹朗读了本书的对话和附录中的地铁广播和安全警示等，杭州万向职业技术学院城市轨道交通运营管理专业团队负责人王叔珩高工和施岳定教授对本书编写工作给予了大力支持并提出了宝贵建议，在此一并表示衷心的感谢。

本书可作为高职院校城市轨道交通运营管理专业或相关专业的教材，也可作为从事城市轨道交通行业员工的培训用书或学习参考。

由于编者水平有限，再加上编写时间较紧，本教材难免有疏漏和不当之处，恳请广大教师和读者批评指正，以便进一步完善。

编 者
2018年9月

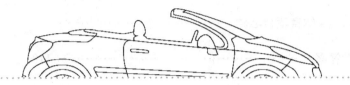

目 录
CONTENTS

Unit 1　Daily Customer Service in Station ⋯⋯⋯⋯⋯⋯⋯⋯⋯⋯⋯⋯ 001
　Lesson 1　Inquiring and Directing ⋯⋯⋯⋯⋯⋯⋯⋯⋯⋯⋯⋯⋯⋯ 001
　Lesson 2　Complaints and Suggestions ⋯⋯⋯⋯⋯⋯⋯⋯⋯⋯⋯⋯ 007
　Lesson 3　Broadcasting ⋯⋯⋯⋯⋯⋯⋯⋯⋯⋯⋯⋯⋯⋯⋯⋯⋯⋯ 013

Unit 2　Ticket Service ⋯⋯⋯⋯⋯⋯⋯⋯⋯⋯⋯⋯⋯⋯⋯⋯⋯⋯⋯⋯ 017
　Lesson 4　Buying Tickets and Checking Tickets ⋯⋯⋯⋯⋯⋯⋯ 017
　Lesson 5　Ticket Machine Failure ⋯⋯⋯⋯⋯⋯⋯⋯⋯⋯⋯⋯⋯⋯ 025
　Lesson 6　Handling Ticket Services in Different Situations ⋯⋯ 029

Unit 3　Subway Security ⋯⋯⋯⋯⋯⋯⋯⋯⋯⋯⋯⋯⋯⋯⋯⋯⋯⋯⋯ 038
　Lesson 7　Security Check ⋯⋯⋯⋯⋯⋯⋯⋯⋯⋯⋯⋯⋯⋯⋯⋯⋯ 038
　Lesson 8　Security Warnings in the Station ⋯⋯⋯⋯⋯⋯⋯⋯⋯ 044
　Lesson 9　Security Warnings on the Platform ⋯⋯⋯⋯⋯⋯⋯⋯ 049

Unit 4　Customer Service in Special Situations ⋯⋯⋯⋯⋯⋯⋯⋯ 055
　Lesson 10　Helping the Sick, the Injured and the Disabled ⋯⋯ 055
　Lesson 11　Lost and Found ⋯⋯⋯⋯⋯⋯⋯⋯⋯⋯⋯⋯⋯⋯⋯⋯ 063
　Lesson 12　Dealing with Emergency ⋯⋯⋯⋯⋯⋯⋯⋯⋯⋯⋯⋯ 070
　Lesson 13　Operating in Adverse Weather ⋯⋯⋯⋯⋯⋯⋯⋯⋯ 076

Unit 5　Customer Service for Big Events ⋯⋯⋯⋯⋯⋯⋯⋯⋯⋯⋯ 081
　Lesson 14　Greetings and Inquiring ⋯⋯⋯⋯⋯⋯⋯⋯⋯⋯⋯⋯ 081
　Lesson 15　The First and Last Train ⋯⋯⋯⋯⋯⋯⋯⋯⋯⋯⋯⋯ 086
　Lesson 16　Public Service ⋯⋯⋯⋯⋯⋯⋯⋯⋯⋯⋯⋯⋯⋯⋯⋯ 091
　Lesson 17　The Asian Games ⋯⋯⋯⋯⋯⋯⋯⋯⋯⋯⋯⋯⋯⋯⋯ 096

Appendix 1　Words and Phrases 单词和短语 ⋯⋯⋯⋯⋯⋯⋯⋯⋯ 102

Appendix 2　Subway Broadcasting 地铁广播 ⋯⋯⋯⋯⋯⋯⋯⋯⋯ 110

Appendix 3	Security Warnings 安全警示	113
Appendix 4	Main Scenic Spots in Hangzhou 杭州市主要旅游景点	115
Appendix 5	Sports Names 体育项目名称	117
Appendix 6	Keys 参考答案	118
Appendix 7	References 参考文献	135

Unit 1

Daily Customer Service in Station

Learning Objectives

In this unit, you will learn:
- how to give directions in a subway station;
- how to deal with different situations;
- how to respond to customers' complaints and suggestions;
- useful phrases and sentences related to broadcasting.

Lesson 1 Inquiring and Directing

I. Warming-up

Task 1: Match the words and expressions with the following pictures.

| a. shopping center | b. exit | c. metro map | d. hospital |

1. _____

2. _____

3. _____

4. _____

Task 2: Have you given directions to others before? If you have, please share your experience.

Task 3: Here is a map of Beijing Subway. You are at Panjiayuan Station（潘家园）, and you want to go to Shichahai Station（什刹海）. How can you get there? Can you describe the route?

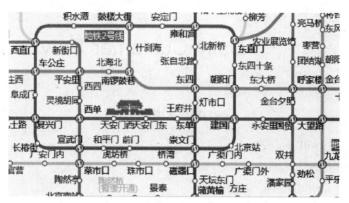

Beijing Subway Map

Number of Subway Lines

II. Situational Dialogues

Dialogue 1

Situation: A foreign passenger is going to take subway to the railway station. He is asking the route and time. (P: Foreign Passenger   E: Metro Employee)

P: Excuse me, how could I get to the East Railway Station?

E: You can take Metro Line 2 at Xueyuan Road, and then transfer to Line 1 at Wulin Square. It will take you to the East Railway Station.

P: How long will it take?

E: About 40 minutes.

P: OK. When is the last train at the transfer stop?

E: Wait for a minute and I'll find it out. The last train of Wulin Square heading for the railway station leaves at 23：12.

P: I see. Thank you very much!

对话1

情景：一位外国乘客需要乘坐地铁到火车站，他正向地铁工作人员询问线路和时间。

（P 为外国乘客　　E 为地铁工作人员）

P：打扰一下，我想去火车东站，您能告诉我怎样去吗？

E：您可以乘坐地铁 2 号线，在学院路上车，在换乘站武林广场站下车，换乘 1 号线，就能到火车东站了。

P：到那里需要多长时间？

E：大概需要 40 分钟。

P：好的。换乘站的末班车到几点？

E：请您稍等，我帮您查查。武林广场站前往火车站方向的末班车是 23 点 12 分。

P：我知道了，非常感谢！

Dialogue 2

Situation：A foreign passenger is going to the First People's Hospital. He is asking the way and time. （P：Foreign Passenger　　E：Metro Employee）

P：Excuse me, I'm going to the First People's Hospital. Which exit should I go?

E：Exit A is the closest.

P：How long will it take to walk there?

E：You can see the hospital when you get out of the metro station.

P：Thanks a lot. Bye!

对话 2

情景：一位外国乘客需要到第一人民医院，他正询问线路和时间。（P 为外国乘客　E 为地铁工作人员）

P：打扰一下，我想去第一人民医院。我该走哪个出口呢？

E：从车站的 A 出口出去最近。

P：出去后还要走多长时间？

E：您出站后就可以直接看到医院了。

P：非常感谢！再见！

Dialogue 3

Situation：A foreign passenger doesn't know how to get to the platform because it's the first time he takes a subway. （P：Foreign Passenger　　E：Metro Employee）

P：Hello, I have bought the ticket, but how could I get to the platform?

E：Go through the entry gate and then you can take the lift to the platform.

P：Thank you!

对话 3

情景：一位外国乘客第一次乘坐地铁，不知道该如何到达站台。（P 为外国乘客　E 为地铁工作人员）

P：您好，我已经买好票了，请问我该从哪里进站？

E：您可以从这边的进站闸机进站，然后乘坐电梯到达站台候车。

P：非常感谢！

Dialogue 4

Situation：A foreign passenger who has missed his stop is asking a metro staff for help. （P：Foreign Passenger　　E：Metro Employee）

P：Good morning. I should have got off at Fengqi Road, but it seems I have missed the stop.

E：Don't worry! You can return to that stop by taking the opposite train. This way, please.

P：OK. What time will the next train arrive?

E：The train will pull in within a minute. It won't take long to get to your destination.

P：Thank you very much!

对话 4

情景：一位外国乘客坐过了车站，下车后寻求车站人员帮助。（P 为外国乘客　　E 为地铁工作人员）

P：您好，我本来要去凤起路站的，但是我好像坐过站了。

E：您别着急。您可以乘坐对向列车返回您要去的车站，请您跟我来。

P：好的，大概要多长时间可以坐上车？

E：列车将在 1 分钟内到站，很快您就能到达您的目的地站。

P：非常感谢！

Words and Phrases

route / ruːt / n. 路线

transfer stop：换乘站

head for：前往

miss the stop：坐过头了

opposite / ˈɒpəzɪt / a. 相反的

pull in：进站

destination / ˌdestɪˈneɪʃn / n. 目的地，终点

Useful Sentences

1. You can take Metro Line 2 at Xueyuan Road, and then transfer to Line 1 at Wulin Square. It will take you to the East Railway Station.

   您可以乘坐地铁 2 号线，在学院路上车，在换乘站武林广场站下车，换乘 1 号线，就能到火车东站了。

2. Excuse me, I'm going to the First People's Hospital. Which exit should I go?

   打扰一下，我想去第一人民医院。我该走哪个出口呢？

3. You can see the hospital when you get out of the metro station.
   您出站后就可以直接看到医院了。
4. I should have got off at Fengqi Road, but it seems I have missed the stop.
   我本来要去凤起路站的,但是我好像坐过站了。
5. You can return to that stop by taking the opposite train.
   您可以乘坐对向列车返回您要去的车站。
6. The train will pull in within a minute.
   列车将在 1 分钟内到站。

III. Exercises

Task 1: Fill in the blanks with the words given in the box. Change the form if necessary.

| route | destination | head for | pull in | opposite |

1. He _____ at the side of the road.
2. The _____ we had planned took us right across Greece.
3. Police attempts to calm the violence had the _____ effect.
4. We arrived at our _____ tired and hungry.
5. If you're indoors, go outdoors. Or _____ the park.

Task 2: Imagine you are a metro employee. A foreign passenger is asking for the way to the restroom. Fill in the blanks according to the Chinese version provided in the brackets. Then act the dialogue out with your partner. (P: Foreign Passenger   E: Metro Employee)

P: Excuse me. 1. _____ (这个站台有洗手间吗)?
E: Sorry, there is no restroom 2. _____ (在这个站台附近). But you can find one 3. _____ (在服务台的后面).
P: How can I get to the information desk?
E: 4. _____ (笔直走) and turn left at the first corner. Then you can 5. _____ (乘电梯到一楼). The information desk is 6. _____ (在电梯的旁边).
P: OK. Thank you so much!

Task 3: Do a role play according to the following situations.

Here is a map of the Hong Kong Mass Transit Railway (MTR). Imagine you are an employee working at Kowloon Station. A foreign passenger is asking you the way to:

1. Central Station
2. Disneyland Resort
3. Airport
4. Mong Kok Station

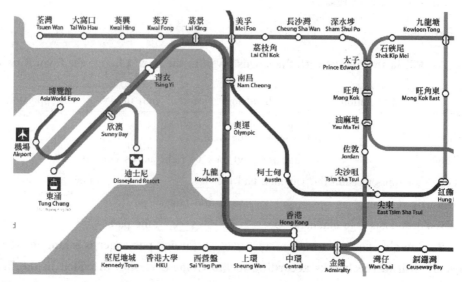

Task 4: Translate the following sentences into English.
1. 到那里非常容易。
2. 您应该在下一站下车。
3. 不好意思打扰一下，这条线到火车站吗？
4. 下一班车什么时候到？
5. 到那里要花多长时间？
6. 您可以先乘 7 号线到静安寺，然后换乘 2 号线到浦东国际机场。

IV. Self-evaluation

	Excellent	Good	Average	Pass	Fail
make conversations with phrases					
participate in pair work and role play					
improve speaking skills					
finish homework independently					
learn the lessons consciously					

3. You can see the hospital when you get out of the metro station.
   您出站后就可以直接看到医院了。
4. I should have got off at Fengqi Road, but it seems I have missed the stop.
   我本来要去凤起路站的，但是我好像坐过站了。
5. You can return to that stop by taking the opposite train.
   您可以乘坐对向列车返回您要去的车站。
6. The train will pull in within a minute.
   列车将在 1 分钟内到站。

III. Exercises

Task 1: Fill in the blanks with the words given in the box. Change the form if necessary.

route	destination	head for	pull in	opposite

1. He _____ at the side of the road.
2. The _____ we had planned took us right across Greece.
3. Police attempts to calm the violence had the _____ effect.
4. We arrived at our _____ tired and hungry.
5. If you're indoors, go outdoors. Or _____ the park.

Task 2: Imagine you are a metro employee. A foreign passenger is asking for the way to the restroom. Fill in the blanks according to the Chinese version provided in the brackets. Then act the dialogue out with your partner. (P: Foreign Passenger   E: Metro Employee)

P: Excuse me. 1. _____ （这个站台有洗手间吗）?
E: Sorry, there is no restroom 2. _____ （在这个站台附近）. But you can find one 3. _____ （在服务台的后面）.
P: How can I get to the information desk?
E: 4. _____ （笔直走） and turn left at the first corner. Then you can 5. _____ （乘电梯到一楼）. The information desk is 6. _____ （在电梯的旁边）.
P: OK. Thank you so much!

Task 3: Do a role play according to the following situations.

Here is a map of the Hong Kong Mass Transit Railway (MTR). Imagine you are an employee working at Kowloon Station. A foreign passenger is asking you the way to:

1. Central Station
2. Disneyland Resort
3. Airport
4. Mong Kok Station

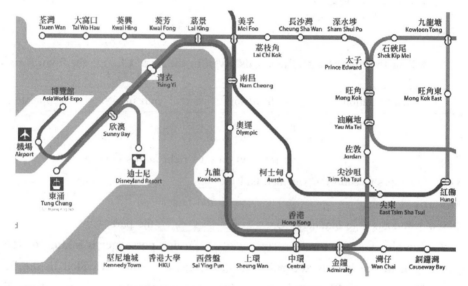

Task 4: Translate the following sentences into English.

1. 到那里非常容易。
2. 您应该在下一站下车。
3. 不好意思打扰一下,这条线到火车站吗?
4. 下一班车什么时候到?
5. 到那里要花多长时间?
6. 您可以先乘7号线到静安寺,然后换乘2号线到浦东国际机场。

IV. Self-evaluation

	Excellent	Good	Average	Pass	Fail
make conversations with phrases					
participate in pair work and role play					
improve speaking skills					
finish homework independently					
learn the lessons consciously					

Lesson 2 Complaints and Suggestions

I. Warming-up

Task 1: Work in pairs and try to describe the impolite manners in the following two pictures.

a

b

Task 2: Have you made a complaint before?

Task 3: Would you give a piece of advice to the subway company in your city?

II. Situational Dialogues

Dialogue 1

Situation: Face to face suggestion. (P: Foreign Passenger   E: Metro Employee)

P: Excuse me. I have some suggestions for you. Would you give me a second?

E: Sure.

P: You see, I'm using electric wheelchair. It's bigger than normal wheelchair. And I can't go through the entry gate. Nowadays, many disabled people use this kind of wheelchair. It's very inconvenient for us to take subway.

E: I'm sorry. Would you please give me more details?

P: For example, it's hard to find a lift at the street level. Often there are no accessibility signs to guide wheelchair users. And some of the lifts are locked. We have to ask staff for help. Besides, many stations don't have any wide-aisle entry gate to allow electric wheelchairs to pass through. Without others' help, I wouldn't be able to take subway alone.

E: I see. I'm sorry for the inconvenience. What you said is true. We do need to improve our wheelchair accessible facilities.

P: Thank you for your listening.

E: Thank you for your valuable suggestions! Have a nice trip.

P: Bye.

对话1

情景：面对面提的意见。（P 为外国乘客　　E 为地铁工作人员）

P：抱歉，我有一些建议，您能给我一些时间吗？

E：当然可以。

P：您看到了，我在用电动轮椅。它比一般的轮椅要大。我根本无法通过进站闸口。现在很多残疾人都在用这种轮椅。对于我们来说，坐地铁太不方便了。

E：我很抱歉，您是否可以说得更具体一些？

P：比如，要在街面上找到进入地铁站的无障碍电梯太难了。通常没有无障碍导向标识来引导使用轮椅的人。而且一些电梯是锁住的，我们得求助工作人员。另外，很多地铁站都没有供电动轮椅通过的进站闸口。没有他人的帮助，我自己根本不可能坐地铁。

E：我明白了，对于您遇到的不便我感到非常抱歉。您说的没错，我们的确有必要改善车站的无障碍设施。

P：谢谢您聆听我的想法。

E：谢谢您的宝贵建议，祝您旅途愉快。

P：再见。

Dialogue 2

Situation: Suggestion from hotline. (P: Foreign Passenger　　E: Metro Employee)

E: Hello, this is the hotline of Hangzhou Metro.

P: Hello, I'm calling to give you some suggestions.

E: Sure. Please go ahead.

P: I hope the air-conditioners on train could be fixed as soon as possible. They don't work effectively in summer, especially when the train is crowded. It's so hot!

E: Yes. What you said is true. We do need to update the air-conditioning system. I'll report your advice to the team leader.

P: OK. Thank you for your time.

E: Thank you for your valuable suggestions.

对话2

情景：通过热线电话提建议。（P 为外国乘客　　E 为地铁工作人员）

E：您好，这里是杭州地铁热线电话。

P：您好，我打电话来提一些建议。

E：好的，您请说。

P：我希望地铁列车上的空调能尽快修一修。它们在夏天无法有效运作，特别是人多拥挤的时候，实在是太热了！

E：您说的没错，我们的确有必要升级空调系统了。我会把您的意见反映给团队负责人。

P：好的，感谢您的宝贵时间。

E：谢谢您的宝贵建议。

Dialogue 3

Situation：A foreign passenger complains about staff's service attitude. (P：Foreign Passenger　E：Metro Employee　　M：Metro Staff at the Customer Service Center)

P：I want to make a complaint. May I talk to someone in charge of the station?

E：Sure. I'm the duty station master. What can I do for you?

P：The attitude of the staff at the Customer Service Center is horrible. I wanted to exchange money. But the staff at the Customer Service Center said "don't you see I'm busy?" in bad attitude, and then he threw the money at the window without saying anything.

E：Madam, don't worry, I will check it.

A few minutes later…

E：Madam, I've checked it. First of all, I extend my sincere apologies to you for the staff's bad service attitude. I have severely criticized his behavior and deducted his performance points. He is also aware of his mistake and will make an apology to you face to face.

M：Madam, I'm sorry for my poor attitude. I will try my best to correct my mistake and please give me another chance. Thank you!

P：I hope this will never happen again.

E：Thank you for your suggestions. We will make efforts to do it well.

对话3

情景：一位外国乘客因工作人员服务态度投诉。(P 为外国乘客　　E 为地铁工作人员　M 为客服中心工作人员)

P：我要投诉。我能和这个车站的负责人谈一谈吗？

E：当然可以。我是这个车站的值班站长。我能为您做些什么吗？

P：刚才客服中心的员工服务态度特别差。我想要兑零，客服中心员工态度恶劣地说"你没看到我正忙着吗？"，之后将零钱扔在窗口，什么也没说。

E：女士，别着急，我先核实情况。

几分钟后……

E：女士，我核实过了。首先我为员工糟糕的服务态度对您表示诚挚的歉意，我已严厉地批评了他的行为并扣除相应的绩效分。该员工也意识到了自己的错误，他会跟您当面致歉。

M：这位女士您好，我为刚才的态度向您说声对不起。我会努力改正，请再给我一次机会，谢谢！

P：希望以后不要再出现这种情况。

E：谢谢您的建议。我们会努力做好的。

Dialogue 4

Situation：A foreign passenger complains about the staff's poor work abilities.

(P: Foreign Passenger   E: Metro Employee)

P: I want to make a complaint. We have queued up for a long time and haven't got the tickets yet. The staff at the Customer Service Center is not familiar with the business at all. She spent too much time in recharging the card.

E: I'm sorry. The staff on duty at the Customer Service Center is a green hand. She is not very familiar with operating the machine. It will be better after one or two days. Please forgive her and don't be angry. We will immediately deploy more staff to the Customer Service Center.

P: I hope you can consider it in advance, the staff's first duty should be equipped with other supporting measures.

E: OK, thank you for your valuable advice. We will try our best.

对话4

情景：一位外国乘客投诉客服中心员工业务差。（P为外国乘客   E为地铁工作人员）

P: 我要投诉，我们排队很长时间还没买到车票，客服中心员工业务一点都不熟，连充值都要花很多时间。

M: 非常抱歉，在客服中心上班的员工是个新手，操作机器还不太熟练，过一两天就好了，请您谅解，别生气，我们立即加派人手到客服中心。

P: 希望你们提前考虑到这些，员工首次上岗要配备其他配套措施。

M: 好的，谢谢您的宝贵建议，我们会努力做好的。

Words and Phrases

electric / ɪˈlektrɪk / a. 电动的

normal / ˈnɔːml / a. 正常的，常规的

accessibility / əkˌsesəˈbɪləti / n. 易接近

aisle / aɪl / n. 过道，通道

pass through: 通过

wheelchair accessible facility: 无障碍设施

hotline / ˈhɒtlaɪn / n. 热线

effectively / ɪˈfektɪvli / ad. 有效地

make a complaint: 投诉

in charge of: 负责，主管

duty station master: 值班站长

extend / ɪkˈstend / v. 给予，提供，发出（邀请等）

severely / sɪˈvɪəli / ad. 严重地，严厉地

criticize / ˈkrɪtɪsaɪz / v. 批评

green hand: 新手

deploy / dɪˈplɔɪ / v. 配置，部署

Useful Sentences

1. I have some suggestions for you. Would you give me a second?
   我有一些建议，您能给我一些时间吗？
2. Would you please give me more details?
   您能再说得详细些吗？
3. Often there are no accessibility signs to guide wheelchair users.
   通常没有无障碍导向标识来引导使用轮椅的人。
4. Besides, many stations don't have any wide-aisle entry gate to allow electric wheelchairs to pass through.
   另外，很多地铁站都没有供电动轮椅通过的进站闸口。
5. Thank you for your valuable suggestions!
   感谢您的宝贵建议！
6. I'll report your advice to the team leader.
   我会把您的建议反映给团队负责人。
7. But the staff at the Customer Service Center said "don't you see I'm busy?" in bad attitude, and then he threw the money at the window without saying anything.
   客服中心员工态度恶劣地说"你没看到我正忙着吗？"，之后将零钱扔在窗口，什么也没说。
8. I have severely criticized his behavior and deducted his performance points.
   我已严厉地批评了他的行为并扣除相应的绩效分。
9. I hope you can consider it in advance, the staff's first duty should be equipped with other supporting measures.
   希望你们提前考虑到这些，员工首次上岗要配备其他配套措施。

III. Exercises

Task 1：Fill in the blanks with the words given in the box. Change the form if necessary.

electric	complaint	complain	accessibility
in charge of	extend		

1. We've received a _____ from one of our listeners about offensive language.
2. You're always _____ !
3. Our _____ bill for July was $115.
4. Someone is put _____ the work.
5. I _____ my heartfelt thanks for your help.
6. Touch-screen voting machines meet the requirements for _____ to people with disabilities.

Task 2: Imagine you are a metro employee. A passenger is giving suggestions about the seats on the platform. Fill in the blanks according to the Chinese version provided in the brackets. Then act the dialogue out with your partner. (P: Foreign Passenger   E: Metro Employee)

P: 1. _____ (我能和车站的负责人谈谈吗)? I would like to give some suggestions.

E: Sure. I'm the duty station master. 2. _____ (有什么我能帮您的)?

P: I hope there will be more seats 3. _____ (在站台上). Every time I come to the platform, there is no vacant seat. 4. _____ (而且，一些座位是破的).

E: Yes. What you said is true. In fact, our company has bought a certain number of chairs, and they will be installed according to the volume and 5. _____ (客流量) in each station.

P: That's great! When will they be installed?

E: 6. _____ (两周内).

P: Perfect! 7. _____ (感谢您的解释).

E: You are welcome. Thank you for your valuable suggestions.

Task 3: Do a role play according to the following situations.

1. A passenger is complaining about the toilet's sanitary conditions (卫生状况).
2. A passenger is complaining about the volume of broadcasting.
3. A passenger is complaining about the bad subway behaviors.

Task 4: Translate the following sentences into English.

1. 我保证相同的情况再也不会发生了。
2. 这是你早应该考虑到的事情！
3. 对于您遇到的不便我感到非常抱歉。
4. 我很抱歉。我们会教育车上的乘客多为他人着想。
5. 我要投诉。
6. 我会立即调派一些维修人员去修理自动售票机。

IV. Self-evaluation

	Excellent	Good	Average	Pass	Fail
make conversations with phrases					
participate in pair work and role play					
improve speaking skills					
finish homework independently					
learn the lessons consciously					

Lesson 3　Broadcasting

I. Warming-up

Task 1: Match the words and expressions with the following pictures.

| a. fire alarm | b. passenger flow | c. broadcast |

1. _____　　2. _____　　3. _____

Task 2: Match the English phrases with their corresponding Chinese meanings.

( )	1. Broadcasting Room	a.	设备故障
( )	2. equipment failure	b.	失物招领处
( )	3. fire drill	c.	广播室
( )	4. Lost and Found Office	d.	盥洗室
( )	5. lavatory	e.	消防演习

Task 3: Can you list three topics that usually appear in subway broadcast?

1. _____
2. _____
3. _____

II. Situational Dialogues

Broadcast 1

Broadcast for a missing person

　　Dear passengers, attention please. We are looking for Wang Yang, a six-year-old boy in yellow coat and blue trousers. If you find him, please send him to the Broadcasting Room. Thank you.

广播 1

寻人广播

亲爱的乘客们,请注意。我们正在寻找一位6岁的男孩,王洋。他身穿黄色外套和蓝色裤子。如果您看到他了,请把他送到广播室来。谢谢。

Broadcast 2

Broadcast for equipment failure

All passengers, attention please! I'm sorry to inform you that the ticket vending machines are not working. Please go to the Customer Service Center to buy tickets or top up. Sorry for any inconvenience it might cause. Thank you for your understanding and cooperation.

广播 2

设施故障广播

各位乘客,请注意。很抱歉通知您,自动售票机停止工作了。请到客户服务中心买票或充值。对此带来的不便我们深表歉意。谢谢您的理解和配合。

Broadcast 3

Broadcast for a fire drill

All passengers, may I have your attention please. This is a fire drill. Please follow the instructions of the staff and leave the station in order immediately. Thank you for your cooperation.

广播 3

消防演习广播

各位乘客,请注意。现在是消防演习。请跟随工作人员的指引立即有序地离开车站。谢谢您的合作。

Broadcast 4

Broadcast for large passenger flow

All passengers, attention please. We are now controlling the passenger flow in our station. Please follow the directions to exit the station. We apologize for any inconvenience it might cause. Thank you for your cooperation.

广播 4

地铁站限制客流量广播

所有乘客,请注意。我站开始限制乘客流量。请跟随指引出站。对此带来的不便我们深表歉意。谢谢您的配合。

Words and Phrases

Broadcasting Room：广播室
failure / ˈfeɪljə (r) / n. 失败，故障
drill / drɪl / n. 训练
fire drill：火警演习
in order：有序地，依次序地

Useful Sentences

1. Dear passengers, attention please.
   各位乘客，请注意。
2. Please go to the Customer Service Center to buy tickets or top up.
   请到客户服务中心买票或充值。
3. Please follow the instructions of the staff and leave the station in order immediately.
   请跟随工作人员的指引立即有序地离开车站。
4. Please follow the directions to exit the station.
   请跟随指引出站。

III. Exercises

Task 1：Fill in the blanks with the words given in the box. Change the form if necessary.

| failure | broadcast | drill | apologize | in order | instruction |

1. Trains may be subject to delay, we _____ for any inconvenience caused.
2. He gave me strict _____ to get there by eight o'clock.
3. The number of business _____ rose steeply last year.
4. I would have soon found the one I wanted if the books had been kept _____.
5. We watched a live _____ of the concert.
6. In some of these schools, army-style _____ are used to instil（灌输）a sense of discipline.

Task 2：Fill in the blanks according to the Chinese version provided in the brackets. Then practice the broadcasts out with your partner.

Broadcast for a lost suitcase

Dear passenger, may I have your attention please. 1. _____ （有哪位乘客丢了行李箱）？Please come to the Lost and Found Office. Thank you.

Broadcast for facility failure

Dear passengers, attention please. 2. _____ （站台附近厕所的门）is broken. Please use the toilet behind the Customer Service Center instead. 3. _____ （对此带来的不便我深表歉意）. Thank you for your understanding and cooperation.

Broadcast for an emergency

All passengers, may I have your attention please. This is an emergency. 4. _____ (车站着火了). Please keep calm and follow the instructions to withdraw the station immediately. 5. _____ (感谢您的配合).

Task 3: Write a broadcast according to the following situations.

1. Broadcast for a missing elder people.
2. Broadcast for a lost passport.
3. Broadcast for a temporarily closed exit.

Task 4: Translate the following sentences into English.

1. 各位乘客,请注意!请不要携带除了导盲犬之外的宠物进站。
2. 请注意列车与站台的空隙。
3. 出站的乘客请注意,因出站闸机故障,请听从工作人员的指引,单程票由工作人员回收,储值票请在下次乘车时到客服中心扣除相应的车资,不便之处,敬请谅解。
4. 各位乘客,请注意。现在车站内的人流量较大,请照顾好您的小孩。
5. 请注意,携带超重行李的乘客请到客户服务中心购买行李票。谢谢您的合作。
6. 亲爱的乘客,请照看好您的行李。无人看管的行李将被移走、销毁。

IV. Self-evaluation

	Excellent	Good	Average	Pass	Fail
make conversations with phrases					
participate in pair work and role play					
improve speaking skills					
finish homework independently					
learn the lessons consciously					

Unit 2

Ticket Service

Learning Objectives

In this unit, you will learn:

- how to buy tickets in different ways;
- how to use Ticket Vending Machines, Add Value Machines and Automatic Gate Machines;
- how to deal with the problems about ticket machine failures;
- how to handle ticket services in a variety of situations;
- useful words and phrases related to ticket service.

Lesson 4 Buying Tickets and Checking Tickets

I. Warming-up

Task 1: Work in pairs to match the words and phrases in the box with the following pictures.

| A. single journey ticket | B. Ticket Vending Machine | C. stored-value card |
| D. automatic gate machine | E. ticket office | F. three-day pass |

1. _____

2. _____

3. _____

4. _____

5. _____

6. _____

Task 2: Can you tell three different ways to buy subway tickets?

1. _____
2. _____
3. _____

Task 3: How does a passenger use a ticket in the subway?

_____
_____

II. Situational Dialogues

Dialogue 1

Situation: A foreign passenger who takes the subway for the first time doesn't know how to buy the ticket. (P: Foreign Passenger　　E: Metro Employee)

P: Excuse me, I am going to East Railway Station, but I don't know how to buy the ticket. Can you tell me how to buy the ticket?

E: You can buy tickets at the ticket office or with the Ticket Vending Machine (TVM).

P: Thank you! There are so many passengers waiting in line at the ticket office. I want to buy a ticket with the TVM. Would you please tell me how to buy a ticket through the TVM?

E: OK. First of all, choose the metro line, and then choose your destination and ticket numbers on the screen, The fare will be showed on the screen. Then put money into the corresponding slot. The TVM only accepts the banknote of 5 yuan and 10 yuan or the coin of 1 yuan. If you don't have change, please exchange them at the ticket office. Finally remember to take your ticket and change from the coin-return at the bottom of the machine.

P: Thank you! By the way, how should I use the ticket?

E: Here is Automatic Gate Machine. Please stand behind the yellow line. Put the ticket on the magnetic area and then you can pass through it as soon as the door opens. Be sure to keep your ticket and we will collect it when you exit the station.

P: Thanks a lot!

E: It's my pleasure. Have a nice trip!

对话1

情景：一位初次乘坐地铁的外国乘客不知如何购票。(P为外国乘客　　E为地铁工作人员)

P：您好，我想去火车东站，不知道如何买票，您能告诉我如何买票吗？

E：您可以到售票处或自动售票机上买票。

P：谢谢！很多人在售票处排队买票，我想在自动售票机上买票，您能告诉我如何在自动售票机上买票吗？

E：好的。首先在屏幕上选择地铁线路和您要去的目的地站，然后选择好购票张数，票款就会显示在屏幕上，然后将零钱投到相应的投币口。自动售票机可以接受5元或

10元的纸币或者1元的硬币。如果没有零钱，请到售票处兑换。最后记住从机器下方的找零处拿到您的票和零钱。

P：谢谢！顺便问一下，如何使用地铁票？

E：这边是自动检票闸机，请站在黄线外，把车票放在磁性区域，闸机门一开你就可以通过了。请收好您的车票，出站时闸机要回收车票的。

P：多谢！

E：这是我的荣幸。祝您旅途愉快！

Dialogue 2

Situation：A foreign passenger who takes the subway for the first time doesn't know how to top up the card through the Add Value Machine. （P：Foreign Passenger　E：Metro Employee）

P：Excuse me, where can I recharge my card?

E：You can recharge your card through the Add Value Machine or at the Customer Service Center.

P：Can you tell me how to top up through the Add Value Machine?

E：Sure. First, select the amount that you need to recharge on the screen. Our Add Value Machine doesn't accept bank card. Please prepare the banknote of 50 yuan or 100 yuan. Please note that the Add Value Machine cannot give change. You should top up on multiples of 50 Yuan. Second, insert the stored-value card into the appropriate slot and then insert the notes into the slot. Finally take out your card after the screen displays a successful recharge.

P：Oh, I've got it. Thanks a lot.

E：It's my pleasure. Have a nice trip!

对话2

情景：一位初次乘坐地铁的外国乘客不知道如何在自助充值机上充值。（P为外国乘客　E为地铁工作人员）

P：请问在哪里充值储值卡？

E：请在自助充值机或客服中心充值。

P：你能告诉我如何在自助充值机上充值吗？

E：当然。首先，在屏幕上选择你要充值的金额，我们的自助充值机暂不支持银行卡充值，请您准备50元或100元的纸币。请注意自助充值机不设找零，请充值50元的倍数。然后，将储值卡放入相应的卡槽内并将纸币投到投币口。最后，屏幕显示充值成功后再将储值卡从卡槽中取出。

P：我明白了，非常感谢。

E：这是我的荣幸。祝您旅途愉快！

Dialogue 3

Situation：A foreign passenger needs to buy a stored-value card. （P：Foreign

Passenger　　E: Metro Employee)

E: Can I help you?

P: I want to buy a stored-value card.

E: OK. You need to pay a deposit of 20 yuan. How much would you like to top up?

P: 150 yuan.

E: OK. Please confirm the amount in your card.

P: Yes, it's correct. By the way, where can I recharge it?

E: You can recharge it at the ticket office or with Add Value Machines in all subway stations.

P: I see. Thanks!

E: You are welcome. Please take your card, change and invoice.

对话 3

情景：一位外国乘客需要购买储值卡。(P 为外国乘客　　E 为地铁工作人员)

E: 要我帮忙吗?

P: 我想买储值票。

E: 好的。您需要支付 20 元押金。您要充值多少?

P: 150 元。

E: 好了。请您确认卡内金额。

P: 没问题。顺便问一下，哪儿能充值?

E: 各个地铁站的售票处和充值机都可以。

P: 知道了，谢谢。

E: 不客气。请收好您的卡、找零和发票。

Dialogue 4

Situation: A foreign passenger asks about the discount for the stored-value card. (P: Foreign Passenger　　E: Metro employee)

P: Can I get the discount if using the stored-value card?

E: You will get 10% off if using the stored-value card to take the subway.

P: It is said that passengers can get the discount if they take the bus by the stored-value card, isn't it?

E: Yes. You are entitled to a benefit of 1 yuan or 2 yuan on the basis of the original 10% off if you transfer to a bus within 90 minutes.

P: Can I get the discount if I take the bus first and then change to subway?

E: Yes, it also applies to bus-to-metro and bus-to-bus transfers, and accumulates over multiple transfers.

P: That's great. Thanks!

对话 4

情景：一位外国乘客询问储值票的折扣。(P 为外国乘客　　E 为地铁工作人员)

P：使用储值卡有折扣吗？

E：使用储值卡乘地铁可以享受九折。

P：听说乘公交车也可以打折，是吗？

E：是的。您在90分钟之内换乘公交车，在原有九折的基础上可以再享受1元或2元优惠。

P：那先乘公交车再乘地铁有优惠吗？

E：是的，这个优惠同样适用于公交车换乘地铁及公交车换乘公交车，而且多次换乘可以享受叠加优惠。

P：这很不错，谢谢！

Dialogue 5

Situation：A foreign passenger doesn't know how to buy a ticket with smartphone.（P：Foreign Passenger　　E：Metro Employee）

P：Excuse me, can you tell me how to buy a ticket?

E：Sure. You can buy a ticket at the ticket office or through the Ticket Vending Machine.

P：Thank you. But I can't operate the machine, it is so complicated.

E：Oh, you can go to the ticket office to buy a ticket.

P：Thank you. Where is the ticket office?

E：It's over there. Please stand in line to buy a ticket.

P：Oh, there are so many people waiting in line. Is there any other way to buy a ticket?

E：Yes. There is a mobile payment device at our station. You can swipe your smartphone and then board the metro train.

P：How can I use my smartphone to pay the fare?

E：You need to download a mobile payment app and get a QR code on your phone. Then you can scan the QR code to enter the station. The price will be deducted from your Alipay account after you swipe to exit the station. I'll show you how to use it. It is simple and convenient. You don't need to bring change to buy a ticket or even carry subway cards.

P：Thank you!

E：You are welcome.

对话5

情景：一位外国乘客不知道如何用智能手机购票。（P为外国乘客　　E为地铁工作人员）

P：打扰一下，你能告诉我如何买票吗？

E：当然可以。你可以在售票处或自动售票机上购票。

P：谢谢。但是我不会操作机器，太复杂了。

E：哦，你可以去售票处买票。

P：谢谢。售票处在哪里？

E：在那边。请排队买票。

P：哦，排队的人太多了。还有别的办法买票吗？

E：是的。我们车站有移动支付设备。你可以刷智能手机乘车。

P：我怎样使用智能手机支付车费呢？

E：你需要下载移动支付应用程序并在手机上获得一个二维码。然后你扫二维码进站。你刷卡出站时车费将从你的支付宝账户中扣除。我来教你如何使用手机购票。这种方法简单方便，你不必带零钱买票，甚至也不用带地铁卡。

P：谢谢！

E：不客气。

Words and Phrases

Ticket Vending Machine：自动售票机

ticket office：售票处

destination / ˌdestɪˈneɪʃn / n. 目的地

corresponding / ˌkɒrəˈspɒndɪŋ / a. 对应的

coin-return：找零处

Automatic Gate Machine：自动检票机，闸机

magnetic / mægˈnetɪk / a. 有磁性的

top up：充值

Add Value Machine：充值机

recharge / ˌriːˈtʃɑːdʒ / v. 充值

Customer Service Center：客服中心

multiple / ˈmʌltɪpl / a. 许多的

stored-value card：储值卡

appropriate / əˈprəʊpriət / a. 适当的

deposit / dɪˈpɒzɪt / n. 押金，存款

confirm / kənˈfɜːm / v. 确认

transfer / trænsˈfɜː (r) / n. 换乘

accumulate / əˈkjuːmjəleɪt / v. 积累

complicated / ˈkɒmplɪkeɪtɪd / a. 复杂的

QR code：二维码

deduct / dɪˈdʌkt / v. 扣除，减去

Useful Sentences

1. The TVM only accept the banknote of 5 yuan and 10 yuan or the coin of 1 yuan.

   自动售票机只接受5元或10元的纸币或者1元的硬币。

2. Finally remember to take your ticket and change from the coin-return at the bottom of the machine.

   最后记住从机器下方的找零处拿到您的票和零钱。

3. Be sure to keep your ticket and we will collect it when you exit the station.

   请收好您的车票，出站时闸机要回收车票的。

4. Can you tell me how to top up through the Add Value Machine?
   你能告诉我如何在自助充值机上充值吗？
5. You need to pay a deposit of 20 yuan.
   您需要支付20元押金。
6. Please confirm the amount in your card.
   请确认卡内金额。
7. You are entitled to a benefit of 1 yuan or 2 yuan on the basis of the original 10% off if you transfer to a bus within 90 minutes.
   如果您在90分钟之内换乘公交车，那么在原有九折的基础上您可以再享受1元或2元优惠。
8. It also applies to bus-to-metro and bus-to-bus transfers, and accumulates over multiple transfers.
   这个优惠同样适用于公交车换乘地铁及公交车换乘公交车，而且多次换乘可以享受叠加优惠。

III. Exercises

Task 1：Fill in the blanks with the words or phrases given in the box. Change the form if necessary.

| transfer | deposit | accumulate | multiple |
| magnetic | destination | top up | confirm |

1. The Greek islands are a favorite _____ for people who enjoy the sun and the sea.
2. The train broke down so we _____ to a bus.
3. 20 is a _____ of 5.
4. Smith _____ as the club's new manager yesterday.
5. A compass needle points to the _____ north pole.
6. In New York City, 1 to 3 inches of snow is expected to _____ before changing to freezing rain tonight.
7. We paid one month's rent in advance, plus a _____ of $500.
8. He had to do extra jobs at the weekend to _____ his income.

Task 2：Fill in the blanks according to the Chinese given in the brackets. Then act the dialogue out with your partner. （P：Foreign Passenger   E：Metro Employee）

Dialogue: A foreign passenger who takes the subway for the first time doesn't know how to exchange money and how to buy a ticket through the TVM.

E：Can I help you?
P：1. _____ （我没零钱）and don't know where to exchange money?
E：You can 2. _____ （到客服中心兑换零钱）.

P: Thank you!

A few minutes later.

P: Excuse me, would you please tell me 3. _____ (如何在自动售票机上买单程票吗)?

E: Certainly. First, you should choose 4. _____ (地铁线路、目的地和车票数量). Wait until the fare is showed on the screen. Second, 5. _____ (把纸币或硬币投入投币口). Finally, 6. _____ (拿走你的车票和找零).

P: What should I do with the ticket?

E: You insert it into the slot at the turnstile and push the turnstile to 7. _____ (进入站台).

P: Thanks a lot. You are so helpful.

E: You are welcome. 8. _____ (旅途愉快).

Task 3: Do a role play according to the different situations.

1. Please help a foreigner who cannot use the TVM to buy a ticket.
2. Introduce how to use the ticket for a foreigner.
3. Help a foreigner who wants to get some change.
4. Explain the discount of a monthly pass to a foreigner who asks about a discount of a ticket.

Task 4: Translate the following sentences into English.

1. 您好,自动售票机只接受5元或者10元或1元硬币,您如果没有零钱,可到客服中心兑换。
2. 对不起,这台自动售票机暂停服务,请选择其他自动售票机购票。
3. 您好,为您充值100元,请确认余额。
4. 您可以从机器下方的找零处取回您的票和零钱。
5. 我们的票价是按照里程计费的。
6. 使用储值卡会有相应的折扣。

IV. Self-evaluation

	Excellent	Good	Average	Pass	Fail
make conversations with phrases					
participate in pair work and role play					
improve speaking skills					
finish homework independently					
learn the lessons consciously					

Lesson 5　Ticket Machine Failure

I. Warming-up

Task 1：Work in pairs to match the English phrases with their corresponding Chinese meanings.

(　　) 1. Ticket Vending Machine　　　A. 半自动售票机
(　　) 2. Customer Service Center　　　B. 出站闸机
(　　) 3. exit gate　　　　　　　　　　C. 自动查询机
(　　) 4. Ticket Checking Machine　　　D. 自动售票机
(　　) 5. entry gate　　　　　　　　　 E. 客服中心
(　　) 6. Booking Office Machine　　　 F. 进站闸机
(　　) 7. Add Value Machine　　　　　 G. 充值机
(　　) 8. Automatic Fare Collection　　H. 自动售检票

Task 2：What does a station employee do when the Ticket Vending Machine doesn't work?

Task 3：How can a passenger exit the subway station when the Automatic Gate Machine is out of service?

II. Situational Dialogues

Dialogue 1

Situation：The coins are jammed in the TVM when a foreign passenger is buying the ticket.
(P：Foreign Passenger　　E：Metro Employee)

P：Excuse me. Why did I insert coins into the machine but no ticket or no refund comes out?

E：Don't worry. Let me check it. Maybe there is something wrong with the TVM. Our staff will solve your problem soon. Please wait for a moment.

E：I'm sorry to keep you waiting for a long time. The coins are jammed in the Ticket Vending Machine. So you should try it again. Here is your money. We apologize for any inconvenience this might cause.

P：That's OK.

对话 1

情景：一位外国乘客购票时出现卡币现象。（P 为外国乘客　　E 为地铁工作人员）

P：您好，为何我投了币，不出票，也没有退钱？

E：别担心，我检查一下。可能是自动售票机出故障了。我们的工作人员马上为您处理。请稍等。

E：抱歉，让您久等了。自动售票机卡币了。请重新购票。这是您刚才购票的钱。不便之处请谅解。

P：没关系。

Dialogue 2

Situation：The TVM is out of service. （P：Foreign Passenger   E：Metro Employee）

E：Good morning. Can I help you?

P：Good morning. Why couldn't I buy ticket through this machine? What's wrong with this machine?

E：Sorry, the TVM is out of service due to the machine failure. I ask the repairman to maintain it. Please choose another machine or buy a ticket at the Customer Service Center. We apologize for any inconvenience this might cause.

P：I can't buy a ticket all the same. Why doesn't the TVM give my change?

E：Sorry, there isn't enough change in the Ticket Vending Machine. I will add the change to it soon. You can use other machines.

P：Thanks.

E：You are welcome.

对话2

情景：车站一台自动售票机暂停服务。（P为外国乘客   E为地铁工作人员）

E：早上好。我能帮您吗？

P：早上好。请问这台机器为何不能购票？怎么了？

E：对不起，由于机器故障，这台自动售票机暂停服务，我马上安排维修人员维修。请选择其他自动售票机或者到客服中心购买车票。给您带来不便，敬请谅解。

P：还是买不了，这台自动售票机怎么不找零钱？

E：对不起，这台售票机零钱不足，我马上补充。您可以使用其他自动售票机。

P：谢谢！

E：不客气。

Dialogue 3

Situation：There is something wrong with all the automatic exit gates at the station. （P：Foreign Passenger   E：Metro Employee）

P：Excuse me. Why can't we go through each gate?

E：Attention please! Due to exit gate failure, you should follow directions from the staff. The single journey tickets should be reclaimed by the staff. Appropriate fare will be deducted from your stored-value card by Customer Service Center when you take the subway next time. Please exit from the side gate. We apologize for any inconvenience this might cause.

对话3

情景：车站全部自动出站闸机出故障了。（P为外国乘客   E为地铁工作人员）

P：您好，为什么每台闸机都出不去？

E：出站的乘客请注意，因出站闸机故障，请听从工作人员的指引，单程票由工作人员回收，储值票请在下次乘车时到客服中心扣除相应的车资。请从边门出站。不便之处，敬请谅解。

Words and Phrases

jam / dʒæm / v. 塞满，卡住
refund / ˈriːfʌnd / n. 退款，偿还
out of service：暂停服务，失效
all the same：仍然，依然
failure / ˈfeɪljə(r) / n. 故障，失败
exchange / ɪksˈtʃeɪndʒ / v. 兑换，交换
reclaim / rɪˈkleɪm / v. 收回，回收
deduct / dɪˈdʌkt / v. 扣除

Useful Sentences

1. Why did I insert coins into the machine but no ticket or no refund comes out?
   为何我投了币，不出票也没有退钱？
2. We apologize for any inconvenience this might cause.
   不便之处，敬请谅解。
3. Sorry, the TVM is out of service due to machine failure. Please choose another one to buy tickets
   对不起，由于机器故障这台自动售票机暂停服务。请选择其他自动售票机购票。
4. Sorry, there isn't enough change in the Ticket Vending Machine. I will add the change to it soon. You can use other machines.
   对不起，这台售票机零钱不足。我马上补充。您可以使用其他自动售票机。
5. Please exit from the side gate.
   请从边门出站。

III. Exercises

Task 1：Fill in the blanks with the words given in the box. Change the form if necessary.

reclaim	deduct	exchange	jam	refund

1. They refused to give me a _____.
2. You may be entitled to _____ some tax.
3. Crowds _____ the entrance to the stadium.
4. The payments _____ from your salary.
5. Where can I _____ my dollars for pounds?

Task 2: Fill in the blanks according to the Chinese given in the brackets. Then act the dialogue out with your partner. (P: Foreign Passenger   E: Metro Employee)

Dialogue A: There is something wrong with the Add Value Machine at the station.

P: Excuse me. Why can't I top up my card through that machine?

E: Sorry, 1. _____ (由于机器故障，充值机暂停服务). I call the repair-man 2. _____ (维修机器). Please choose another machine or 3. _____ (到客服中心充值). We apologize for any inconvenience this might cause.

Dialogue B: The tickets are jammed in the TVM when a foreign passenger is buying the ticket.

P: Excuse me. Why did I insert coins into the TVM but no ticket comes out?

E: We apologize for any inconvenience this might cause. Our staff will 4. _____ (马上为你处理问题). Please wait for a moment.

E: I'm sorry 5. _____ (让你久等了). The ticket is jammed in the machine. 6. _____ (请重新购票). Here is your money. We apologize for any inconvenience this might cause.

P: That's OK.

Task 3: Do a role play according to the following situation.

Suppose you are a station operator. You see a foreigner buying a ticket with the TVM. But the TVM doesn't work when he inserts a note of 20 yuan into the machine. He is very puzzled. Please help solve the problem and help him buy a ticket.

Task 4: Translate the following sentences into English.

1. 打扰一下，我刚刚把单程票投入回收口但闸机没开。
2. 请在单上签名，我给您发张免费出站票。
3. 这台自动售票机暂停服务，请到另一台售票机上去购单程票。
4. 可能是机器出故障了。

IV. Self-evaluation

	Excellent	Good	Average	Pass	Fail
make conversations with phrases					
participate in pair work and role play					
improve speaking skills					
finish homework independently					
learn the lessons consciously					

Lesson 6 Handling Ticket Services in Different Situations

I. Warming-up

Task 1: Work in pairs and write down the English words or phrases according to the given chinese.

A. non-registered card	B. failure	C. overtravel	D. no entry record
E. corresponding fare	F. overtime	G. expired ticket	H. magnetic card
I. ticket conductor	J. no exit record	K. irregular ticket	L. invalid ticket

1. 相应车资   _____
2. 不记名卡   _____
3. 无效票   _____
4. 过期票   _____
5. 超时   _____
6. 超程   _____
7. 故障   _____
8. 磁卡   _____
9. 票务员   _____
10. 车票异常   _____
11. 无进站记录   _____
12. 无出站记录   _____

Task 2: Would you explain some possible reasons if a passenger cannot get into the station with his ticket?

Task 3: Would you explain some possible reasons if a passenger cannot get out of the station with his ticket?

II. Situational Dialogues

Dialogue 1

Situation: A foreign passenger has overstayed at the station, now he is in the paid area and cannot exit the station. (P: Foreign Passenger   E: Metro Employee)

P: Excuse me. Why can't I exit the station by this ticket?

E: Please wait for a moment. Let me check it for you.

After seconds...

E: Well, the computer shows that the departure station of your ticket is Fengqi Road and the destination is East Railway Station. And this station is Qibao. The ticket shows that you've overtraveled. So that is the reason why you can't exit the station.

P: Oh, what should I do then?

E: You can exit the station after you pay the appropriate fare for the overtravel.

P: How much should I pay for the overtravel?

E: RMB 2 yuan

P: All right.

E: Thank you. Your ticket has been updated. Now you can exit the station with this ticket, Bye.

P: Thanks!

对话1

情景：一位外国乘客车票超程，在付费区，不能出站。（P 为外国乘客　　E 为地铁工作人员）

P: 您好，这张票为什么无法出站？

E: 请您稍等，我帮您看看。

几秒后……

E: 您好，电脑显示您的车票出发站是凤起路，您的目的地是火车东站，而这站是七堡，您的车票显示超程，这就是您不能出站的理由。

P: 哦，那我该怎么办？

E: 您需要补交相应的超程车资方可出站。

P: 补多少钱？

E: 人民币2元。

P: 好的。

E: 谢谢，已经帮您处理完毕，您可以持这张票出站了，再见。

P: 谢谢！

Dialogue 2

Situation: A foreign passenger stayed at the station overtime, now he is in the paid area and cannot exit the station. (P: Foreign Passenger　　E: Metro Employee)

P: Excuse me. Why can't I exit the station by this ticket? What's wrong with my ticket?

E: Could you please show me your ticket?

P: Certainly. Here you are.

After seconds...

E: Well, how long did you stay at the station?

P: More than 3 hours, I think. I was waiting for my friend at the station.

E: Your ticket shows that you have stayed at the station overtime.

P: What is overtime?

E: According to the related metro ticketing rules, you can stay at the station with the ticket within 180 minutes. The period beyond 180 minutes is called overtime.

P: Oh, sorry, I didn't know that.

E: You may refer to the notes at the back of your ticket for this time limit.

P: What should I do then?

E: You need to pay the extra fee for the overtime and then you can exit the station.

P: How much should I pay for the overtime?

E: RMB 3 yuan.

P: All right.

E: I charge you 3 yuan and have finished updating your ticket. Now you can exit the station with this ticket. Bye.

P: Thanks!

对话2

情景：一位外国乘客车票超时，在付费区，不能出站。（P 为外国乘客　　E 为地铁工作人员）

P：您好，这张票为什么出不了站？我的车票怎么了？

E：能让我看看您的车票吗？

P：当然，给您。

几秒后……

E：您好。您在车站待了多久？

P：我想3个多小时吧。我在车站等朋友。

E：您的车票显示超时。

P：什么是超时？

E：根据相关地铁票务规定，您持票进站后超过180分钟后出站，属于超时。

P：哦，对不起，我不知道那个规定。

E：地铁票的背面有相关的规定。

P：那我该怎么办？

E：您需要补相应的超时车资方可出站。

P：补多少钱？

E：人民币3元。

P：好的。

E：收您3元，已经帮您处理完毕，您可以持这张票出站，再见。

P：谢谢！

Dialogue 3

Situation: A foreign passenger has swiped his card when entering the station, but he can't go into the station. He has stayed in the non-paid area for no more than 20 minutes. (P: Foreign Passenger　　E: Metro Employee)

P: Excuse me. I just swiped my card but I couldn't enter the station.

E: Please wait for a moment. Let me check it for you.

E: Your card shows that there is an entrance record on it and it hasn't been over 20 minutes till now. I will update your card. Please wait for a moment.

P: All right.

E: Your card has been updated, you can enter the station with the card, please bring your card.

P: Thanks!

对话3

情景：一位外国乘客进站时已刷卡但是不能进站，在非付费区，未超过20分钟。（P为外国乘客　E为地铁工作人员）

P：您好，我刚刚刷了卡但不能进站。

E：请稍等，我帮您看看。

E：您好，您的车票显示有进站记录，刷卡到现在未超过20分钟，我会帮您处理。请稍等。

P：好的。

E：已经帮您更新，您可以持这张票进站了，请收好您的车票。

P：谢谢！

Dialogue 4

Situation: A foreign passenger cannot enter the station with his stored-value card. He is now in the non-paid area and his card had an entrance record the other day. (P: Foreign Passenger　E: Metro Employee)

P: Excuse me. Why can't I enter the station?

E: Please wait for a moment. Let me check it for you.

E: Well, your ticket showed that you didn't swipe your card when exiting the station yesterday. So you can't enter the station. As required we need to deduct your minimum fare of 2 yuan.

P: All right.

E: Your card has been updated, please take your stored-value card. Have a nice trip.

P: Thanks!

对话4

情景：一位外国乘客所持储值票无法进站，在非付费区，有非当日进站记录。（P为外国乘客，E为地铁工作人员）

P：您好，为什么我无法进站？

E：请稍等，我帮您看看。

E：您好，您的车票显示昨天进站后出站未刷卡，所以今天无法正常进站，根据规定我们要扣除您的最低车资2元。

P：好的。

E：已经帮您处理好了，请收好您的储值卡。祝您旅途愉快！

P：谢谢！

Dialogue 5

Situation: A foreign passenger has an invalid ticket or expired ticket. He is in the non-paid area and his ticket should be reclaimed. (P: Foreign Passenger   E: Metro Employee)

P: Excuse me. Why can't I enter the station?

E: Please wait for a moment. Let me check it for you.

E: Well, your ticket has been invalid or expired. Please check if you take the wrong ticket.

P: I only have this ticket.

E: According to the related metro ticketing rules, we need to reclaim invalid tickets or expired tickets. Please buy a ticket again. Thank you for your cooperation.

P: I just bought the ticket from the TVM over there. Why is it invalid?

E: Please wait for a moment. Our clerk will check it for you soon.

E: Sorry, an invalid ticket is issued from the TVM. You can get the refund at the Customer Service Center. Please buy a single journey ticket again. We apologize for any inconvenience this might cause.

P: Well, that's OK!

对话5

情景：一位外国乘客所持车票是无效票或者过期票，在非付费区，需要回收车票。（P为外国乘客   E为地铁工作人员）

P：您好，为什么我无法进站？

E：请稍等，我帮您看看。

E：您好，您的车票显示为无效票（或过期票），您看看是否拿错车票了。

P：我只有这一张车票。

E：根据相关地铁票务规定，我们需要回收无效票（或过期票）。请您另行购票。多谢配合。

P：我刚刚是从那边的自动售票机上购买的，怎么会是无效票？

E：请稍等，我们的工作人员马上帮您核实。

E：非常抱歉自动售票机发售了一张无效车票。您可到客服中心拿回退款。请您重新购买一张单程票。给您造成不便，敬请谅解！

P：好的，没关系！

Dialogue 6

Situation: There is no magnetism in a foreign passenger's stored-value card, so he can't enter the station. He is in the non-paid area and needs to replace his card. (P: Foreign Passenger   E: Metro Employee)

P: Hello, I can't enter the station.

E: Don't worry. I will deal with it immediately.

E: Your card has no magnetism and there is no ticket information in the machine. Customer Service Center is not responsible for ticket magnetization. Please go to Caihong Card Company to deal with it. We apologize for any inconvenience this might cause.

P: Where is the Caihong Card Company?

E: Well, you can take the Line 2 and get off at Wulinmen Station and then get out of the station from exit A. You can't miss it.

P: Well, thank you!

对话6

情景：一位外国乘客储值卡无磁性，无法进站，在非付费区，需要更新票卡。（P为外国乘客　　E为地铁工作人员）

P：您好，我无法进站。

E：别着急，我马上帮您处理。

E：您的这张票卡没有磁性了，机器上无法查看车票信息，客服中心不负责车票的充磁，您需要到彩虹卡公司去处理。不便之处，敬请谅解。

P：彩虹卡公司在哪里？

E：您可以乘坐地铁2号线到武林门站，然后从A出口出站就能找到彩虹卡公司了。

P：好的，谢谢！

Dialogue 7

Situation: A foreign passenger lost his ticket and asked the station employee for help. (P: Foreign Passenger　　E: Metro Employee)

P: Excuse me. I lost my ticket. What can I do?

E: Well, according to the related rules, you need to buy it again and pay for the ticket cost. If it is a stored-value card, the card is non-registered. You have to apply for a new one.

P: But I really lost the ticket. I have bought the ticket.

E: I'm sorry. The missing ticket should be dealt with in accordance with this rule, according to the related ticketing rules.

P: All right. I'll buy the ticket again. By the way, if my ticket is broken, can I replace it?

E: Yes, you can bring your ticket and receipt to replace it at the Customer Service Center.

对话7

情景：一位外国乘客丢失车票，寻求车站工作人员帮助。（P为外国乘客　　E为地铁工作人员）

P：打扰一下，我的车票丢了，怎么办？

E：您好。根据有关规定，车票丢失，需要重新购买并支付车票的工本费。如果储值票丢失，它是不记名的，你得再申请一张新卡。

P：但是我真的丢了，我买过票了。

E：非常抱歉，票务相关规定要求丢失车票必须按照此规定执行。

P：好的，那我再补一张票吧。顺便问一下，如果票坏了，可以换吗？

E：可以拿着车票、收据到客服中心换。

Words and Phrases

paid area：付费区

departure station：出发站

overtravel / ˈəʊvətrævəl / n. 超程

update / ˌʌpˈdeɪt / v. 更新

overtime / ˈəʊvətaɪm / ad. 超出时间地

refer to：参考

extra / ˈekstrə / a. 额外的

swipe / swaɪp / v. 刷（卡）

non-paid area：非付费区

invalid ticket：无效票

expired ticket：过期票

issue / ˈɪʃuː / v. 发行，发表

magnetism / ˈmæɡnətɪzəm / n. 磁性

magnetization / ˌmæɡnətɪˈzeɪʃən / n. 磁化

non-registered / nɒn ˈredʒɪstəd / a. 不记名的

in accordance with：按照

receipt / rɪˈsiːt / n. 收据

Useful sentences

1. The ticket shows that you've overtraveled. You can exit the station after you pay the appropriate fare for the overtravel.

   您的车票显示超程，需要补交相应的超程车资方可出站。

2. Your ticket has been updated.

   您的车票已经更新好了。

3. According to the related metro ticketing rules, you can stay at the station with the ticket within 180 minutes. The period beyond 180 minutes is called overtime.

   根据相关地铁票务规定，您持票进站超过 180 分钟后出站，属于超时。

4. Your card shows that there is an entrance record on it and it hasn't been over 20 minutes till now.

   您的车票显示有进站记录，刷卡到现在未超过 20 分钟。

5. We need to deduct your minimum fare of 2 yuan.

   我们需要扣除您的最低车资 2 元。

6. We need to reclaim invalid tickets or expired tickets.

   我们需要回收无效票或过期票。

7. Your card has no magnetism.

   您的卡没有磁性了。

8. If it is a stored-value card, the card is non-registered.

   假如是储值卡的话，它是不记名的。

Ⅲ. Exercises

Task 1: Fill in the blanks with the words or phrases given in the box. Change the form if necessary.

| swipe | update | register | refer to |
| overtime | in accordance with | extra | expire |

1. You need to _____ your card to get in the building.
2. All the local newspapers should _____ with the municipal authorities.
3. Guests at this hotel can use the gym at no _____ cost.
4. When does your driving license _____?
5. Our advice may contain a grain of truth for you to _____.
6. The feedback from the computer enables us _____ the program.
7. We should make decisions _____ specific conditions.
8. He was exhausted after working _____ for several nights running.

Task 2: Fill in the blanks according to the Chinese given in the brackets. Then act the dialogue out with your partner. (P: Foreign Passenger   M: Metro Employee)

Dialogue A: A foreign passenger has swiped his card when entering the station, but he cannot enter the station. He has stayed in the non-paid area for more than 20 minutes.

P: Excuse me. I just swiped my card but I couldn't enter the station.

E: Please wait for a moment. Let me check it for you.

E: Your card shows that 1. _____ (卡里有一次进站记录). It has been for more than 20 minutes 2. _____ (从刷卡到现在). According to the subway ticketing rule, we need to 3. _____ (回收您的卡). Please buy it again. 4. _____ (谢谢合作).

P: All right.

Dialogue B: A foreign passenger has a stored-value card with no exit information, he is in the non-paid area and needs to update his card.

P: Hello, I can't enter the station.

E: Don't worry. 5. _____ (我马上处理).

E: Your ticket shows that 6. _____ (上次乘车无出站记录). Please tell me 7. _____ (上次乘车在哪站出站的?)

P: Wulinmen Station.

E: Well, your card has been updated, and now 8. _____ (您可以正常使用了).

P: Thank you!

Task 3: Do a role play according to the different situations.

1. Please help a foreigner who couldn't get out of the station because he stayed at the station more than 3 hours.
2. Please help a foreigner who couldn't exit the station because he traveled over the distance.
3. Please help a foreigner who couldn't get into the station because his card has no magnetism.
4. Please help a foreigner who couldn't enter the station because of insufficient balance in his card.
5. Please help a foreigner replace his card because his card doesn't work.

Task 4: Translate the following sentences into English.

1. 您的车票已超时，需要补超时车费。
2. 您的单程票已经有进闸记录，而且进闸时间至现在已经超过了20分钟，根据票务规则，我们需要回收此单程票。
3. 您的车票是无效票，请重新购买。
4. 您的卡没有磁性了，我们可以给您调换新卡。
5. 请您在收据上填写您的姓名和电话号码。

IV. Self-evaluation

	Excellent	Good	Average	Pass	Fail
make conversations with phrases					
participate in pair work and role play					
improve speaking skills					
finish homework independently					
learn the lessons consciously					

Unit 3

Subway Security

Learning Objectives

In this unit, you will learn:
- the signs of security in the subway;
- the basic security regulations;
- useful words and phrases related to security warnings and reminders;
- how to deal with emergent situations.

Lesson 7 Security Check

I. Warming-up

Task 1: Work in pairs and look at the following security signs. Discuss them with your partner and match them with the phrases in the box.

a. no smoking	b. handheld metal detector	c. no pets	d. no leaning
e. X-Ray scanner	f. no eating and drinking	g. walk-through metal detector	

1. _____ 2. _____ 3. _____

4. _____ 5. _____ 6. _____ 7. _____

Task 2: Can you list three items that are prohibited at subway stations?

1. _____
2. _____
3. _____

Task 3: Work in pairs. Describe the following two pictures and figure out passengers' wrong behavior.

     a   b

a. _____
b. _____

II. Situational Dialogues

Dialogue 1

Situation: A metro employee is persuading a foreign passenger to go through the security check. (P: Foreign Passenger E: Metro Employee)

E: Good morning, sir. Would you please put your bag on the belt and go through the security check?

P: Why? There's nothing dangerous.

E: Sir, for your and others' safety, every passenger should go through the security check. It's your duty and also our responsibility.

P: I'm in a hurry, and so many people are queuing up! It's too time-consuming!

E: Sorry, sir. The security check will only take a minute or two. Look, the queue is moving fast! Please put your bag on the belt of the X-ray scanner. It will take longer time if you don't cooperate.

P: OK then!

E: Thank you for your cooperation!

对话1

情景：一名工作人员正在说服一位外国乘客配合安检。（P 为外国乘客　　E 为地铁工作人员）

E：早上好。先生。请把您的包放在传送带上通过安检，好吗？

P：为什么？我又没带危险物品。

E：可是，先生，为了您和他人的安全，每位乘客都需要通过安检。这也是您的义务、我们的职责。

P：我赶时间，这么多人排队！安检太浪费时间了！

E：对不起，先生，安检只会占用您一两分钟的时间。看，队伍移动得很快！把您的包放在X光扫描机的传送带上就可以了。如果您不配合，可能更浪费您的时间。

P：好吧！

E：谢谢您的配合！

Dialogue 2

Situation：A foreign passenger with a pet is refused entry to the subway. (P：Foreign Passenger　　E：Metro Employee)

E：Good morning, madam. According to the regulations, pets are not permitted on the subway.

P：Oh, I didn't see any notice!

E：There are significant signs all over eye-catching positions in the subway station, and we also announce the regulations through the broadcast.

P：But I have already bought a ticket.

E：No problem, we'll give you a refund.

P：Can I leave my pet here? And I'll pick it up when I come back.

E：Sorry, madam. We can't keep personal belongings for passengers according to the regulations. So it's better for you to take other means of transportation.

P：OK!

E：Thanks for your cooperation!

对话2

情景：一位外国乘客因为携带宠物而未通过安检。(P为外国乘客　　E为地铁工作人员)

E：上午好，女士。按照地铁相关规定，地铁车站禁止携带宠物进站。

P：噢，我没看到提示！

E：进站后的每个醒目位置我们都有显著的提醒标识，我们车站也有广播提醒。

P：我票都买好了。

E：没问题，我们可以给您退票。

P：那我能把宠物寄存在你这里吗？我回来再取。

E：对不起，女士，车站规定不负责保管乘客的私人物品。您还是选择其他交通工具较妥当！

P：好吧！

E：谢谢您的配合！

Dialogue 3

Situation：A metro employee is persuading a foreign passenger that she could not take balloons into the station. (P: Foreign Passenger　　E: Metro Employee)

E: Good morning, madam. Inflated balloons are forbidden in the metro station. I'm afraid you have to release the air!

P: I'm sorry. I thought there's nothing dangerous to take a balloon.

E: It's really dangerous to take a balloon into the station. It may fly onto the contact net, causing the train to stop. Balloons are also likely to explode on the subway which will lead to a panic or a stampede.

P: OK then!

E: Thanks for your cooperation!

对话3

情景：一名工作人员正在说服一位外国乘客不可携带气球进站。（P为外国乘客　　E为地铁工作人员）

E：早上好，女士。地铁车站禁止携带气球进站，请您将气球放气处理！

P：抱歉，我以为气球没有危险。

E：携带气球乘车危险性极高。气球有可能会飞到我们车站的接触网上造成列车停运，还有可能在乘车时候发生爆炸引起恐慌，造成踩踏等危险情况。

P：好吧！

E：谢谢您的配合！

Dialogue 4

Situation: A passenger with a durian is refused entry into the subway. (P: Foreign Passenger　E: Metro Employee)

E: Good morning, madam. You can't take durian into the subway.

P: Why?

E: According to the regulations, anything dangerous or smelly is banned on the subway. Moreover, a durian with shell can be dangerous because it may injure people in a crowded train. Please be cooperative. Thank you!

P: OK!

对话4

情景：一位外国乘客被劝阻带榴莲进站。（P为外国乘客　　E为地铁工作人员）

E：上午好，女士。很抱歉，榴莲不能带入地铁。

P：为什么？

E：根据规定，乘客不可携带危险性、异味物品进站。带壳的榴莲也属于危险物品，在列车拥挤的情况下很容易刺伤他人。请您配合我们的工作，谢谢！

P：好吧！

Words and Phrases

persuade / pəˈsweɪd / v. 说服，劝说
security check：安检
go through：经过，通过
responsibility / rɪˌspɒnsəˈbɪləti / n. 责任，义务
queue up：排队等候
time-consuming / ˈtaɪm kənˈsjuːmɪŋ / a. 耗时的
permit / pəˈmɪt / v. 允许
significant / sɪɡˈnɪfɪkənt / a. 显著的，有意义的
eye-catching position：醒目位置
announce / əˈnaʊns / v. 宣布，播报
personal belongings：个人物品
balloon / bəˈluːn / n. 气球
inflated / ɪnˈfleɪtɪd / a. 充了气的，膨胀的
forbidden / fəˈbɪdn / a. 被禁止的，严禁的
release / rɪˈliːs / v. 释放
contact net：接触网
explode / ɪkˈspləʊd / v. 爆炸
lead to：导致
panic / ˈpænɪk / n. 恐慌
stampede / stæmˈpiːd / n. 惊跑，人群的蜂拥
durian / ˈdʊəriən / n. 榴莲
smelly / ˈsmeli / a. 有臭味的
be banned：被禁止
cooperative / kəʊˈɒpərətɪv / a. 合作的

Useful Sentences

1. Would you please put your bag on the belt and go through the security check?
   请您把您的包放在传送带上通过安检，好吗？
2. It will take longer time if you don't cooperate.
   如果您不配合，可能更浪费您的时间。
3. There are significant signs all over eye-catching positions in the subway station, and we also announce the regulations through the broadcast.
   进站后的每个醒目位置我们都有显著的提醒标识，我们车站也有广播提醒。
4. We can't keep personal belongings for passengers according to the regulations.
   车站规定不负责保管乘客的私人物品。

5. It may fly onto the contact net, causing the train to stop. Balloons are also likely to explode on the subway which will lead to a panic or a stampede.

   气球有可能会飞到我们车站的接触网上造成列车停运，还有可能在乘车时候发生爆炸引起恐慌，造成踩踏等危险情况。

6. According to the regulations, anything dangerous or smelly is banned on subway.

   根据规定，乘客不可携带危险性、异味物品进站。

III. Exercises

Task 1: Fill in the blanks with the words given in the box. Change the form if necessary.

| persuade | time-consuming | permit | forbidden |
| release | lead to | panic | cooperative |

1. He was fairly easily _____.
2. Reducing speed limits should _____ fewer deaths on the roads.
3. I asked them to turn down their music, but they're not being very _____.
4. Some of the more _____ jobs can now be done by machines.
5. The security system will not _____ you to enter without the correct password.
6. _____ spread through the crowd as the bullets started to fly.
7. Coal（煤）power stations _____ sulphur dioxide（二氧化硫）into the atmosphere.
8. The use of cameras in this museum is strictly _____.

Task 2: Imagine you are a metro employee. A foreign passenger with a durian in her suitcase is not willing to go through the security check. Fill in the blanks according to the Chinese version provided in the brackets. Then act the dialogue out with your partner. （P: Foreign Passenger   E: Metro Employee）

E: Good morning, madam. 1. _____（请把您的行李箱放在传送带上通过安检）?

P: Why? There's nothing dangerous in my suitcase.

E: Security check is to 2. _____（保证您的安全）. Every passenger 3. _____（有义务通过安检）.

P: OK. Sure. 4. _____（我应该怎么做）?

E: Put your suitcase on the belt and you also need to go through the metal detector.

P: OK.

E: Sorry, madam. 5. _____（您能把行李箱打开吗）?

P: What's wrong?

E: It seems that there is a durian in your suitcase.

P: Yes. It's a gift for my father.

E: 6. _____ (根据规定), anything smelly is banned on the subway. You'd better 7. _____ (把它扔掉或者选择其他交通方式).

P: Sorry, I didn't know. I will take a taxi instead.

E: 8. _____ (感谢您的合作).

Task 3: Do a role play according to the following situations.

1. Persuade a passenger to go through the security check.
2. Persuade a passenger not to take fireworks into the subway station.
3. Persuade a passenger not to take a bike into the subway station.
4. Explain the security regulations to a foreign passenger.

Task 4: Translate the following sentences into English.

1. 安检是为了确保地铁上所有乘客的安全。
2. 安检只需要花费一两分钟时间。乘客只需把包或行李放到X光扫描仪的传送带上就可以了。
3. 车站不负责保管旅客的私人物品。
4. 严禁携带易爆、易燃的危险物品乘车。
5. 根据规定,有异味的物品不可携带进站。
6. 气球可能会在地铁上爆炸,从而引起恐慌,造成踩踏等危险情况。

IV. Self-evaluation

	Excellent	Good	Average	Pass	Fail
make conversations with phrases					
participate in pair work and role play					
improve speaking skills					
finish homework independently					
learn the lessons consciously					

Lesson 8 Security Warnings in the Station

I. Warming-up

Task 1: Work in pairs and match the English words or phrases with their corresponding Chinese meanings.

(　　) 1. escalator　　　　　　　　a. 吸烟区

(　　) 2. smoking zone　　　　　　b. 消防设备

(　　) 3. emergency stop button　　c. 自动扶梯

(　　) 4. firefighting equipment　　d. 香烟

(　　) 5. cigarette　　　　　　　　e. 紧急停止按钮

Task 2: **Can you list three safety reminders you've heard in subway stations**?

1. _____
2. _____
3. _____

II. Situational Dialogues

Dialogue 1

Situation: A foreign passenger with a child is going to take the escalator. (P: Foreign Passenger   E: Metro Employee)

E: For your safety, elders and children are better to take the lift.

P: Where is the lift?

E: Please follow me and I'll take you there.

P: Thank you!

P: Excuse me, would you please help me to take the luggage? It's too heavy.

E: Sure! No problem.

P: Thanks a lot!

E: That's what we should do. Have a nice trip! Bye!

对话1

情景：一位带小孩的外国乘客正要坐自动扶梯。（P 为外国乘客   E 为地铁工作人员）

E：老人和小孩请乘坐垂直电梯，这样比较安全。

P：垂直电梯在哪里？

E：请您跟我走，我带您过去。

P：谢谢。

P：不好意思，能帮我把行李提一下吗？太重了。

E：当然．没问题。

P：太感谢了！

E：这是我们应该做的。祝您旅途愉快。再见。

Dialogue 2

Situation: A foreign passenger is smoking in the station. (P: Foreign Passenger   E: Metro Employee)

E: Sir, there is no smoking zone in the station. Would you please drop your cigarette in the dustbin after putting it out?

P: I'm sorry. OK!

E: Thank you for your cooperation.

对话2

情景：一位外国乘客正在车站吸烟。（P为外国乘客　　E为地铁工作人员）

E：先生，地铁车站内没有设专门的吸烟区。请您把烟掐灭后扔到垃圾桶内。

P：不好意思。好的！

E：谢谢您的配合。

Dialogue 3

Situation：Children are playing and running in a metro station.（P：Foreign Passenger　　E：Metro Employee）

E：Good morning, madam. Please take care of your children. It's really dangerous for children to play and run in the station. For security reasons, please ask them to stop chasing. Thank you!

P：OK. Thank you for your warning!

对话3

情景：孩子们在车站内嬉戏打闹。（P为外国乘客　　E为地铁工作人员）

E：女士，您好！请您看管好您的孩子。小朋友在地铁站内嬉戏打闹很危险。为了安全起见，请您劝阻您的孩子，谢谢！

P：好的。谢谢您的提醒！

Dialogue 4

Situation：A child pressed the Escalator Emergency Stop Button.（P：Foreign Passenger　　E：Metro Employee）

E：Good morning! The Escalator Emergency Stop Button could only be pressed under emergency, or it will cause a fall-off of other people. Please take care of your child.

P：I'm sorry!

对话4

情景：一位小朋友按了扶梯紧急停梯按钮。（P为外国乘客　　E为地铁工作人员）

E：早上好！扶梯的紧急停梯按钮是在紧急的情况才可以使用的。如果误按，会造成严重的乘客摔伤事故。请看管好您的孩子。

P：不好意思！

Dialogue 5

Situation：A foreign passenger used the firefighting equipment under a non-emergency circumstance.（P：Foreign Passenger　　E：Metro Employee）

E：Sir, this is the firefighting equipment in our station. You can open the seals and use it only when there is an emergency. Would you please put it back, or the police will come and take care of this situation.

P：I'm sorry. I'll put it back.

对话 5

情景：一位外国乘客在非紧急情况下使用了消防设备。（P 为外国乘客　E 为地铁工作人员）

E：先生，这个是车站的消防设备，只有在紧急的情况下才可以破封使用，请您放回原位。如果您不配合，公安人员会到现场进行处理。

P：不好意思，我会把它放回去的。

Words and Phrases

escalator / ˈeskəleɪtə（r）/ n. 自动扶梯
lift / lɪft / n. 垂直电梯
for your safety：为了您的安全
luggage / ˈlʌgɪdʒ / n. 行李
smoking zone：吸烟区
cigarette / ˌsɪgəˈret / n. 香烟
put out：熄灭
chase / tʃeɪs / v. 追赶，追逐
Escalator Emergency Stop Button：扶梯紧急停梯按钮
firefighting / ˈfaɪəfaɪtɪŋ / n. 消防，灭火
circumstance / ˈsɜːkəmstəns / n. 环境，情况
seal / siːl / n. 密封，封条

Useful Sentences

1. For your safety, elders and children are better to take the lift.
   老人和小孩请乘坐垂直电梯，这样比较安全。
2. Would you please drop your cigarette in the dustbin after putting it out?
   您能把烟掐灭后扔到垃圾桶内吗？
3. The Escalator Emergency Stop Button could only be pressed under emergency, or it will cause a fall-off of other people.
   扶梯的紧急停梯按钮是在紧急的情况才可以使用的。如果误按，会造成严重的乘客摔伤事故。
4. You can open the seals and use it only when there is an emergency.
   只有在紧急的情况下才可以破封使用。

III. Exercises

Task 1：Fill in the blanks with the words given in the box. Change the form if necessary.

| escalator | luggage | put out | chase | circumstance | seal |

1. Don't bother about me! _____ the fire first.
2. I'll meet you by the up _____ on the second floor.
3. Clean the _____ around the fridge door regularly so that it remains airtight（密封的）.
4. Never leave your _____ unattended（没人照看，无人看管）.
5. Obviously we can't deal with the problem until we know all the _____.
6. The police car was going so fast, it must have been _____ someone.

Task 2: Imagine you are a metro employee. An elder foreign passenger carrying over size luggage is going to use the escalator. Persuade him to use a lift instead and help him with his luggage. Fill in the blanks according to the Chinese version provided in the brackets. Then act the dialogue out with your partner. (P: Foreign Passenger   E: Metro Employee)

E: Excuse me, sir. 1. _____（为了您的安全）, please use the lift if you have over size luggage.

P: 2. _____（直升电梯在哪里）?

E: Follow me please. I'll take you there.

P: Thank you very much.

E: Here it is. 3. _____（需要我帮您提行李吗）?

P: Yes, please. It's too heavy.

E: No problem. Oh! Wait a moment! Why do you 4. _____（按下电梯紧急停止按钮）?

P: I'm so sorry. I touch it by mistake.

E: The lift emergency stop button 5. _____（只有在紧急情况下才可以按）, or it may cause an accident. It is really dangerous to do so.

P: OK. I will be careful next time.

E: I'll have to reset the lift. 6. _____（请稍等一会儿）.

P: OK. Sorry about that.

Task 3: Do a role play according to the following situations.

1. Stop the fight between two passengers in the station.
2. Stop children from chasing on the escalator.
3. Stop children from playing the firefight equipment in the station.

Task 4: Translate the following sentences into English.

1. 禁止在车站追逐打闹。
2. 搭乘扶梯时请握紧扶手靠右站稳。
3. 未经允许，不得擅自触动车站内的消防设备。
4. 您不应该这样做，扶梯的紧急停梯按钮是在紧急的情况才可以使用的。
5. 请不要破坏地铁车站设备。
6. 地铁站内禁止吸烟。

IV. Self-evaluation

	Excellent	Good	Average	Pass	Fail
make conversations with phrases					
participate in pair work and role play					
improve speaking skills					
finish homework independently					
learn the lessons consciously					

Lesson 9 Security Warnings on the Platform

I. Warming-up

Task 1: Look at the following pictures of the subway platforms in different cities. Discuss them with your partner and try to guess the names of the cities.

1. _____   2. _____

3. _____   4. _____

Task 2: Discuss with your partner and figure out the function of the yellow line in the picture.

Task 3: Work in pairs. Describe the following two pictures and figure out passengers' wrong behavior.

a   b

a. _____

b. _____

II. Situational Dialogues

Dialogue 1

Situation: No photographing, please! (P: Foreign Passenger   E: Metro Employee)

E: Sir, photographing is not allowed in this metro station.

P: Why?

E: All the equipment here is in secret. Moreover, the flash light will damage our signaling equipment.

P: I see. Sorry!

E: Thank you for your cooperation!

对话1

情景：请勿拍照！（P为外国乘客 E为地铁工作人员）

E：先生，本地铁站内不允许拍照！

P：为何？

E：地铁车站所有设备均属于机密。其次，您拍照使用的闪光灯会损坏我们的信号设备。

P：我明白了。不好意思。

E：谢谢您的配合。

Dialogue 2

Situation: Please wait for the next train. (P: Foreign Passenger E: Metro Employee)

E: Sir, the doors of this train are closing. Please wait for the next train for your safety!

P: But I'll be late for work!

E: The next train will come in two minutes. You will be hurt if you force the door to get on the train.

P: OK then!

对话 2

情景：请等待下一班列车。(P 为外国乘客 E 为地铁工作人员)

E：先生，列车即将关门。为了您的安全，请您等待下一班列车！

P：但是我上班要迟到了！

E：下一班列车两分钟就能到站。您如果冲门上车，可能会被屏蔽门夹伤。

P：那好吧！

Dialogue 3

Situation: Please get off the Part Route and transfer to another train! (P: Foreign Passenger E: Metro Employee)

E: Sir, this is the final stop of this train since it is a Part Route. Please transfer at the opposite if you want to continue traveling.

P: What is a Part Route?

E: A Part Route is an additional train running in rush hours to relieve the passenger flow pressure. It runs between Chengzhan Railway Station and East Railway Station, so this is our final stop and all the passengers should get off the train.

P: Oh, I see. I'll get off the train.

E: Thanks for your cooperation.

对话 3

情景：小交路清客，请换乘其他车辆。(P 为外国乘客 E 为地铁工作人员)

E：先生，本趟列车运行的是小交路，该站为终点站，如果您要继续乘车，请您到对面站台换乘。

P：什么叫小交路？

E：小交路就是在高峰时段为了缓解客流压力，地铁运营公司加开的列车，加开的路段为城站火车站到火车东站，所以到这个终点站我们需要清客。

P：噢，我明白了。马上下车。

E：谢谢您的配合。

Dialogue 4

Situation: A foreign passenger dropped his wallet onto the tracks and he attempts to pick it up by himself. (P: Foreign Passenger　　E: Metro Employee)

E: Sir, what are you doing!

P: My wallet dropped onto the tracks. And I just want to pick it up.

E: It's really dangerous for you to do so. You may be hurt by the tracks, or even be killed by the train. Moreover, your behavior will disturb the operation of the train and lead to a serious accident!

P: OK. I see. But what should I do now?

E: We will pick it up for you after the last train stops operating in the evening. Please leave your name and phone number. I'll contact you after your wallet has been picked up.

P: Thanks a lot.

E: You are welcome.

对话4

情景：一位外国乘客的钱包掉落到了轨道上，他试图自行将其捡起。（P 为外国乘客　E 为地铁工作人员）

E：先生，您在做什么！

P：我的钱包掉到铁轨上了，我只是想把它捡起来。

E：您这样做太危险了。您可能被铁轨弄伤，甚至被列车撞死。此外，您的行为还会干扰列车运行，造成严重的事故。

P：好吧，我知道了。但是我现在该怎么办？

E：我们会在晚上末班车停运之后替您把它拾起来。请留下您的姓名和电话号码，钱包拾起来之后我会马上联系您。

P：非常感谢！

E：不客气。

Words and Phrases

photograph / ˈfəʊtəɡrɑːf / v. 拍照

in secret：机密

moreover / mɔːrˈəʊvə (r) / ad. 而且，此外

damage / ˈdæmɪdʒ / v. 损坏

signaling equipment：信号设备

Part Route：小交路

final stop：终点站

additional / əˈdɪʃənl / a. 附加的，额外的

rush hour：交通拥堵时间，高峰期

relieve / rɪˈliːv / v. 减轻

passenger flow：客流量

pressure / ˈpreʃə(r) / n. 压力

attempt to do sth.：尝试做某事

Useful Sentences

1. Photographing is not allowed in this metro station.
   本地铁站内不允许拍照。
2. Moreover, the flash light will damage our signaling equipment.
   其次，您拍照使用的闪光灯会损坏我们的信号设备。
3. Please transfer at the opposite if you want to continue traveling.
   如果您要继续乘车，请您到对面站台换乘。
4. A Part Route is an additional train running in rush hours to relieve the passenger flow pressure.
   小交路就是在高峰时段为了缓解客流压力，地铁运营公司加开的列车。
5. Moreover, your behavior will disturb the operation of the train and lead to a serious accident!
   此外，您的行为还会干扰列车运行，造成严重的事故。

III. Exercises

Task 1：Fill in the blanks with the words given in the box. Change the form if necessary.

photograph	moreover	pick up	damage
additional	relieve	attempt to	pressure

1. Teachers are under increasing _____ to work longer hours.
2. The earthquake caused great _____.
3. He enjoys selling and, _____, is good at it.
4. He made no _____ conceal his dislike of me.
5. She was given a shot of morphine (吗啡) to _____ the pain.
6. I prefer _____ people rather than places.
7. He _____ his cap _____ from the floor and stuck it back on his head.
8. There will be an extra charge for any _____ passengers.

Task 2：Imagine you are a metro employee. There are two kids playing and running near the tracks. Fill in the blanks according to the Chinese version provided in the brackets. Then act the dialogue out with your partner. (P：Foreign Passenger E：Metro Employee K：Kid)

E：Sir, 1. _____ (在铁轨附近玩耍或追逐是非常危险的). Please take care of your children.

P: 2. _____ （抱歉，我不知道）.

E: They may be hurt by the train, or even 3. _____ （摔落到轨道上）. For safety reasons, please stand behind the yellow safety line.

P: OK. 4. _____ （感谢你的提醒）. Hey, boys. Stop chasing!

K: Papa, my toy car drops onto the tracks. 5. _____ （您能帮我捡回来吗）?

E: Sir, it will be very dangerous for you to pick up the toy car. We can do it for you after the last train 6. _____ （停止运行） in the evening.

P: Thank you so much!

E: 7. _____ （这是我们应该做的）. Have a nice trip!

Task 3: Do a role play according to the following situations.

1. A passenger drops his bank card onto the tracks.
2. A passenger falls onto the tracks by accident.
3. A passenger rushes to get on the train.

Task 4: Translate the following sentences into English.

1. 请不要在地铁站内拍照。
2. 请不要超越黄色安全线。
3. 终点站到了，如果您要继续乘车，请您到对面站台换乘。
4. 请不要在站内嬉戏打闹。
5. 请照顾好您的小孩。
6. 请注意列车与站台的空隙。

IV. Self-evaluation

	Excellent	Good	Average	Pass	Fail
make conversations with phrases					
participate in pair work and role play					
improve speaking skills					
finish homework independently					
learn the lessons consciously					

Unit 4

Customer Service in Special Situations

Learning Objectives

In this unit, you will learn:
- how to help the sick, the injured and the disabled friendly;
- how to handle the problem about passengers' lost and found;
- how to deal with emergencies;
- how to deal with train operating in the adverse climate;
- useful words and phrases related to customer service in special situations.

Lesson 10   Helping the Sick, the Injured and the Disabled

I. Warming-up

Task 1: Work in pairs to match the words and phrases in the box with the following pictures.

| A. wheelchair | B. barrier free passage | C. headache |
| D. heatstroke | E. heart attack | F. broken arm |

1. _____

2. _____

3. _____

4. _____

5. _____

6. _____

Task 2: As a metro employee, how do you take care of a heatstroke passenger?

Task 3: As a metro employee, how do you help a disabled passenger in a wheelchair travel by subway?

II. Situational Dialogues

Dialogue 1

Situation: An employee helped a foreign passenger who felt dizzy in the weather of high temperature. (P: Foreign Passenger   E: Metro Employee)

E: Madam, what's the matter with you?

P: I feel dizzy. The weather is too hot. I feel like suffering from heat-stroke.

E: Why don't you have a rest? You can take the subway when you feel better. Can I send you to an air conditioned room now?

P: Thank you very much.

The staff member helps carry the woman to an air-conditioned room, and sponges her down with cold water.

E: Please sit in the chair and have a rest. Here is some water and cooling ointment. You will surely feel better after using them.

A few minutes later…

E: How do you feel now?

P: I feel much better. Your service is so good! Thank you very much.

E: You are welcome.

对话1

情景：一位地铁工作人员帮助高温天气感觉头晕的外国乘客。（P为外国乘客   E为地铁工作人员）

E：这位女士，您怎么了？

P：我觉得头晕，天气太热了，我好像中暑了。

E：您先休息一会吧，等身体感觉好了再坐车。我扶您到空调休息室吧？

P：非常感谢！

这位工作人员扶着那位女士到空调房间，用冷毛巾为她降温。

E：请坐在椅子上休息一下，这是水和清凉油，使用后您肯定会感觉好点。

几分钟之后……

E：你现在感觉怎么样？

P：好多了，你们的服务实在太好了！非常感谢！

E：不客气。

Dialogue 2

Situation: A foreign passenger felt uncomfortable because of hypoglycemia and sought for help from a station employee. The employee took the candy and brown sugar water to the scene immediately. (P: Foreign Passenger   E: Metro Employee)

E: Madam, what's wrong with you?

P: I feel tired and my body feels weak. I haven't had breakfast, and I have hypoglycemia.

E: We have prepared some brown sugar water and candy for you, which have a good effect on relieving your hypoglycemia.

P: Thank you very much.

E: You had better have a rest at the moment. You can take the subway when you feel better. We suggest you should go to hospital in time if you don't feel well. We will be at your service.

P: Thank you. I feel much better after drinking the brown sugar water and can continue to take the subway. Don't worry about me.

E: OK, do you need any other help?

P: No, thank you!

E: You are welcome.

对话2

情景：一位外国乘客因低血糖感觉不舒服，寻求车站工作人员帮助。一位工作人员立即带上糖果和红糖水到现场。（P为外国乘客   E为地铁工作人员）

E: 女士，请问哪里不舒服？

P: 我感到很疲倦，身体感到很虚弱，我没吃早餐，我有低血糖。

E: 我们准备了红糖水和糖果，对缓解低血糖有很好的效果。

P: 非常感谢。

E: 您现在最好休息一下，等身体感觉好些了再乘车。如果身体感觉不好，我们建议您及时就医。我们会随时为您服务。

P: 谢谢。喝了红糖水后我感觉好多了，可以继续乘车，不用担心。

E: 好的，还需要其他帮助吗？

P: 不用了，谢谢！

E: 不客气。

Dialogue 3

Situation: A foreign passenger didn't hold the handrail and fell from the escalator and was hurt. An employee pressed the emergency button immediately. (P: Foreign Passenger   E: Metro Employee)

E: Don't be afraid, madam. We will immediately call 120 for you. Could you please tell me where you were hurt?

P: My right leg and right arm were hurt.

E: How did it happen? Did anybody push you?

P: No. I didn't hold the handrail and lost balance and then fell from the escalator.

E: Oh, we have a first-aid kit. We'll help you with your wound simply.

P: Thank you. Please contact my friend, and her telephone number is 13805714539.

E: OK, we will inform your friend immediately.

P: Thanks.

对话3

情景：一名外国乘客未抓紧扶手而从电梯上摔下来，车站工作人员立即按压紧急停梯按钮。（P 为外国乘客　　E 为地铁工作人员）

E：女士，您别怕，我们立即叫120。请告诉我您哪里受伤了？

P：我的右腿和右手臂受伤了。

E：怎么发生的？有人推你吗？

P：没有，我没抓紧扶手，失去平衡，从自动扶梯上摔下来了。

E：哦，我们有急救箱，先帮您简单处理一下伤口。

P：谢谢！请马上给我朋友打电话，她的电话号码是13805714539。

E：好的，我们会立即通知您的朋友。

P：谢谢。

Dialogue 4

Situation: Five passengers took the elevator and were trapped in it due to the elevator malfunction. (P: Passenger　　E: Metro Employee)

P: Staff? Five people were trapped in the elevator.

E: Don't worry. We will rush to the scene immediately.

E: Please keep calm and do not attempt to open the elevator door. Our professional maintenance personnel have already taken the tools and will arrive here soon.

P: I was a bit dizzy after coming out finally.

E: What can I do for you?

P: Give me a cup of hot water. I'm going to rest for a while.

E: OK, we are sorry for the elevator malfunction.

P: I hope you will have a good check on your equipment.

E: Thank you for your comments. We will improve our service in time and welcome your suggestions.

对话4

情景：5位乘客乘坐垂直电梯，电梯故障导致乘客被困电梯。（P 为乘客　　E 为地铁工作人员）

P：工作人员吗？我们5个人被困在电梯里了。

E：别担心，我们立即赶到现场。

E：请各位保持冷静，千万不要强行拉开电梯门。我们专业的维修人员已经拿好工具，马上就到。

P：终于出来了，我有点头晕。

E：我能为您效劳吗？

P：给我一杯热水，我要休息一会。

E：好的，今天的电梯故障我们非常抱歉。

P：希望你们好好检查设备。

E：谢谢您的意见，我们会及时改进服务，欢迎你们多提建议。

Dialogue 5

Situation：A foreign passenger in a wheelchair at the subway station entrance wants to take the subway. (P：Foreign Passenger   E：Metro Employee)

E：Hello, sir. Can I help you?

P：I want to take the subway, but there is no lift and barrier free passage near the entrance, which causes great inconvenience to my trip.

E：Sorry, don't worry. Our staff will help you immediately.

P：I hope you can report the facilities inadequacy to your superiors.

E：Sure, our superiors have also attached great importance to this problem and managed to solve it. I think there will be a big improvement in the future.

P：I hope so.

E：Let's help you to get to the platform to wait for the train, and wish you a pleasant journey.

P：Thank you very much!

E：You are welcome. It's my pleasure.

对话5

情景：一位在地铁车站入口处的坐轮椅的外国乘客想乘坐地铁。（P为外国乘客   E为地铁工作人员）

E：您好，先生，我能帮您吗？

P：我要乘车，这入口处附近没设垂直电梯和无障碍通道，给我的出行带来了极大的不便。

E：抱歉，您别担心，我们工作人员马上帮您。

P：希望你向上级反映设施不足的问题。

E：一定，上级部门也非常重视并设法解决这个问题，我想以后会有很大改进的。

P：希望如此。

E：我们帮您抬到站台候车，祝您旅途愉快。

P：非常感谢！

E：不客气，我很乐意。

Dialogue 6

Situation：A foreign passenger is discussing barrier free facilities at the station with a metro employee. (P：Foreign Passenger   E：Metro Employee)

P：Sorry, I'm using an electric wheelchair, which is larger than the ordianry ones. I just cannot go through the gate at all.

E: I will take you to the side door and then you can go through it.

P: Many disabled people use electric wheelchairs nowadays. They are so wide and heavy that cannot be lifted even by several people. It is very inconvenient for us to travel by subway.

E: I'm sorry. Would you please give some specific examples?

P: For example, it's difficult for me to find an accessible elevator at the street level. Usually, there are no accessibility signs or the signs are not clear enough to guide wheelchair users. Some elevators are not in normal use and I always need to ask the staff for help. I hope you can report these facility inadequacies to your superiors.

E: I see, I feel very sorry for your inconvenience. You're right. We do need to improve the barrier free facilities at the station.

P: Thank you for listening to my suggestions. The train is coming. I have to go.

E: Thank you for your suggestions, and wish you to have a nice trip.

P: Goodbye.

对话6

情景：一位外国乘客与地铁工作人员探讨地铁车站无障碍设施问题。（P 为外国乘客 E 为地铁工作人员）

P：对不起，我用的是电动轮椅，比一般轮椅要大，根本无法通过这个闸机。

E：我带您走边门通过。

P：现在很多残疾人使用电动轮椅，很宽也很重，几个人根本抬不动，我们坐地铁非常不方便。

E：非常抱歉，您能说具体点吗？

P：比如我很难从街面上找到无障碍电梯。通常没有无障碍导向标识，或者导向很不清楚，缺乏引导功能。有些电梯不能正常使用，得求助工作人员，希望你向上级反映车站设施的不足。

E：我明白了，给您带来不便，我感到非常抱歉。您说得没错，我们的确有必要改善车站的无障碍设施。

P：谢谢您聆听我的想法，列车快来了，我得走了。

E：谢谢您的意见，祝您旅途愉快。

P：再见。

Words and Phrases

dizzy / ˈdɪzi / *a.* 晕眩的

heat-stroke / ˈhiːtstrəʊk / *n.* 中暑

sponge / spʌndʒ / *v.* 用海绵（或湿布）擦洗

cooling ointment：清凉油

hypoglycemia / ˌhaɪpəʊglaɪˈsiːmiə / *n.* 低血糖症

scene / siːn / *n.* 现场，场面

relieve / rɪˈliːv / v. 缓解，减轻
at sb. 's service：愿为某人服务
handrail / ˈhændreɪl / n. 扶手
emergency button：紧急按钮
first-aid kit：急救箱
trap / træp / v. 陷入（困境），设圈套
malfunction / ˌmælˈfʌŋkʃn / n. 故障，失灵
lift / lɪft / n. 电梯
barrier free passage：无障碍通道
attach importance to：重视
accessible elevator：无障碍电梯
accessibility / əkˌsesəˈbɪləti / n. 可接近性，可达性

Useful Sentences

1. What's the matter with you? / What's wrong with you?
   你怎么了？
2. Here is some water and cooling ointment.
   这是水和清凉油。
3. How do you feel now?
   你现在感觉怎样？
4. My body feels weak.
   我感到很虚弱。
5. How did it happen? Did anybody push you?
   怎么发生的？有人推你吗？
6. I didn't hold the handrail and lost balance and then fell from the escalator.
   我没抓紧扶手，失去平衡，从自动扶梯上摔下来了。
7. Five people were trapped in the elevator.
   5个人被困在电梯里了。
8. Please keep calm and do not attempt to open the elevator door. Our professional maintenance personnel have already taken the tools and will arrive here soon.
   请各位保持冷静，千万不要强行拉开电梯门。我们专业的维修人员已经拿好工具，马上就到。
9. I hope you will have a good check on your equipment.
   我希望你们好好检查设备。
10. There is no lift and barrier free passage near the entrance, which causes great inconvenience to my trip.
    这入口处附近没设垂直电梯和无障碍通道，给我的出行带来了极大的不便。
11. I hope you can report the facilities inadequacy to your superiors.
    我希望你向上级反映设施不足的问题。

12. It's difficult for me to find an accessible elevator at the street level.
    我很难从街面上找到无障碍电梯。

III. Exercises

Task 1: Fill in the blanks with the words or phrases given in the box. Change the form if necessary.

| relieve | sponge | trap | at sb.'s service |
| malfunction | dizzy | scene | attach importance to |

1. It's so nice to _____ myself down in a hot bath, it makes me feel so much cleaner.
2. There was no evidence of technical _____.
3. Climbing so high made me feel _____.
4. If you need anything, I am _____.
5. The route was designed _____ traffic congestion.
6. They _____ in the burning building.
7. The _____ of the novel is set in Scotland.
8. The government should _____ subway security.

Task 2: Fill in the blanks according to the Chinese given in the brackets. Then act the dialogue out with your partner. (P: Foreign Passenger   M: Metro Employee)

Dialogue A: A foreign passenger got a sudden heart attack at the station, an employee helped him.

E: 1. _____ (先生，您还好吗)? Can you hear me? 2. _____ (您随身携带药了吗)?

P: I have a heart attack. 3. _____ (我现在喘不过气来了). The medicine is in my bag.

E: OK. 4. _____ (我马上给您拿药), please hold on.

E: Do you feel better now after taking the medicine? 5. _____ (要我通知您的家人吗)?

P: No. 6. _____ (吃了药我感觉好多了). Thank you for your help.

E: You are welcome.

Dialogue B: A foreign passenger rushed to get off the subway train and was hurt by the platform screen door, an employee helped him.

P: 7. _____ (我被门夹伤了), please help me.

E: I will help you right now. You don't have to worry about.

E: Are you okay?

P: 8. _____ (我的手臂动不了). I think my arms must be cut off.

E: 9. _____ (我们马上帮您叫救护车) and our staff will 10. _____

_____ （陪您去医院）.

P: All right.

Task 3: Do a role play according to the following situations.

1. Help a foreigner who had a bad headache in the subway station.
2. Help a foreigner in a wheelchair get into the station and get on the train.
3. A foreigner had a heart attack in the subway station, but he was still conscious. Suppose you are a metro employee, you should provide first aid and call an ambulance for him.
4. Help a little foreign girl who fell off the escalator and broke her arm.

Task 4: Translate the following sentences into English.

1. 急救人员应将中暑病人带到有空调的房间，并用冷水为其降温。
2. 对不起，我朋友不舒服，他有心脏病，您可以帮忙叫辆救护车吗？
3. 我休息一下就没事了。
4. 对不起，我坐着轮椅如何进站乘车？
5. 我觉得左手腕很痛，可能骨折了。

IV. Self-evaluation

	Excellent	Good	Average	Pass	Fail
make conversations with phrases					
participate in pair work and role play					
improve speaking skills					
finish homework independently					
learn the lessons consciously					

Lesson 11　Lost and Found

I. Warming-up

Task 1: Work in pairs to match the words and phrases in the box with the following pictures.

A. passport	B. briefcase	C. key	D. ring
E. ID Card	F. umbrella	G. phone	H. Lost and Found Office

1. _____　2. _____　3. _____　4. _____

5. _____ 6. _____ 7. _____ 8. _____

Task 2: What should you do if you lose something important at the subway station?

Task 3: How do you express your thanks if someone helps you find the lost?

II. Situational Dialogues

Dialogue 1

Situation: A foreign passenger lost her handbag on the subway and she worried about it. She was reporting it to an employee. (P: Foreign Passenger   E: Metro Employee)

P: Sorry, I had left my handbag in the train.

E: Oh, I'm sorry to hear that. Can you tell me the time and direction of that train?

P: Well, the train has just pulled out of the station. It's bound for Lin Ping.

E: OK, could you please describe your handbag as detailedly as possible?

P: Well, it is a yellow handbag with rectangular lattice.

E: What's in it?

P: There are a lot of important files, and my purse in it.

E: Yes. Is it on the seat or under it?

P: It is on the seat.

E: OK, we'll call the clerk in the next stop to look for it at once. If you are in a hurry, you can leave your contact information, we will inform you later.

P: All right. My name is Mary Green and my number is 15067893485.

E: Please keep the phone open, we will contact you the moment we find it.

P: Thank you.

E: You are welcome.

对话1

情景：一位外国乘客在地铁上遗失了手提包，很着急，正向工作人员报失。（P为外国乘客   E为地铁工作人员）

P：打扰一下，我把手提包落在列车上了。

E：哦，我很遗憾。请问那趟列车的时间和方向？

P：好的，就是刚刚开走的那趟列车，开往临平的。

E：哦，您能尽可能详细地描述一下您的手提包吗？

P：好的，这是一只长方格的黄色手提包。

E：包里有什么？

P：包里有很多重要文件，还有我的钱包。

E：包放在座位上还是在座位下面？

P：在座位上。

E：好的，我们马上打电话叫下一站工作人员寻找。如果您赶时间的话，也可以留下您的联系方式，我们稍后通知您。

P：好的。我是玛丽·格林，我的电话号码是15067893485。

E：请保持手机畅通，我们一找到手提包就与您联系。

P：谢谢！

E：不客气。

Dialogue 2

Situation：A foreign passenger is claiming the lost luggage at the Customer Service Center.（P：Foreign Passenger   E：Metro Employee）

P：Hello, I'm here to get my lost luggage!

E：Yes, please tell me when you lost your luggage and what items were in it.

P：Sure, my luggage is lost on the platform around nine o'clock in the morning. There are some clothes, my diploma and other important items in it.

E：Yes, could you please show me your identity card or passport?

P：Yes, here is my passport.

E：Oh. This is your luggage. Please check the items in it and fill out this form and sign your name here.

P：Sure. No problem.

E：A passenger found your luggage on the platform.

P：How kind he is! Thank you.

E：You are welcome.

对话2

情景：一位外国乘客正在客服中心认领行李箱。（P 为外国乘客   E 为地铁工作人员）

P：您好，我来这里取我丢失的行李箱。

E：好的，请您告知我遗失行李箱的时间及行李箱内的物品。

P：可以。我的行李箱大概早上九点落在站台上的。行李箱内有几件衣服、毕业证书和其他重要物品。

E：好的，请出示您的身份证或者护照，好吗？

P：好的，这是我的护照。

E：哦，这是您的行李箱。请核对行李箱内的物品，并填写这张表，在这儿签名。

P：好的，没问题！

E：有一名乘客在站台上发现您的行李箱的。

P：他真的太好了！谢谢你！

E：不客气。

Dialogue 3

Situation: A foreign passenger was looking for his identity card. (P: Foreign Passenger   E: Metro Employee)

P: Excuse me. Could you help me?

E: Sure. What's wrong?

P: I have lost my ID card. I wonder if anyone has turned in one.

E: I'm afraid not. We haven't received any ID card today. When did you notice that your ID card was lost?

P: Well, it's around 11:00 a.m. When I was having lunch in a restaurant, I found that my ID card had been lost. I could not find it anywhere in my bag. I remember that the last place I used it today was in this station.

E: Where did you use ID card in this station exactly?

P: Near the Ticket Vending Machine.

E: OK. Don't worry. I'll call the relevant departments to check if they've found an ID card. Would you please leave your name and contact number? I'll contact you after I get the information.

P: Sure. My name is Zhang Rong. Here is my name card. Thank you so much!

E: You are welcome.

对话3

情景：一位外国乘客正在寻找丢失的身份证件。(P为外国乘客   E为地铁工作人员)

P：对不起，您能帮我吗？

E：当然可以。怎么了？

P：我身份证丢了。不知道是否有人捡到上交？

E：恐怕没有。我们今天没有收到身份证。您什么时候发现您的身份证丢了？

P：哦，大约上午十一点左右。当我在餐厅吃午饭的时候，我发觉身份证丢了。我找遍了整个包都找不到。我记得今天最后一次用身份证就在这个车站。

E：您到底在车站的什么地方用身份证的？

P：在自动售票机附近。

E：好的，别着急。我会联系有关部门，看看是否有人捡到身份证。您能留下姓名和联系方式吗？一有消息我就会联系您。

P：当然。我叫张荣。这是我的名片。非常感谢！

E：不客气

Dialogue 4

Situation: A foreign passenger was looking for a missing child. (P: Foreign Passenger   E: Metro Employee)

P: Excuse me, sir. Would you help me?

E: Sure. What can I do for you?

P: My son is lost. I can't find him after I come out of the washroom.

E: Calm down, madam. Can you write down his name, age, appearance, and your name? I can look for him through the radio system.

P: His name is Wang Yang, and he is 6 years old. He is wearing a yellow coat and blue trousers. My name is Li Hong. And this is my contact number.

E: OK. Let's wait for the good news.

P: Thank you so much for your help!

E: You are welcome.

对话4

情景：一位外国乘客正在寻找走失的小孩。（P 为外国乘客　　E 为地铁工作人员）

P：不好意思，先生。您能帮我吗？

E：当然可以。我能为您做些什么吗？

P：我儿子走丢了。我从洗手间出来就没见到他了。

E：女士，请冷静下来。您能写一下您孩子的姓名、年龄、外貌特征和您的名字吗？我可以通过广播找他。

P：他叫王洋，今年6岁。他穿了黄色外套和蓝色裤子。我叫李红，这是我的联系电话。

E：好的，让我们等待好消息吧！

P：非常感谢您的帮助。

E：不客气。

Words and Phrases

pull out of：离开，驶离

be bound for：开往，准备到……去

rectangular / rekˈtæŋgjələ(r) / a. 矩形的，长方形的

lattice / ˈlætɪs / n. 格子；格状物

purse / pɜːs / n. 钱包

the moment：一……就……

claim / kleɪm / v. 认领，索取

diploma / dɪˈpləʊmə / n. 文凭

identity card：身份证

fill out：填写

turn in：上交

exactly / ɪgˈzæktli / ad. 确切地，完全地

relevant / ˈreləvənt / a. 相关地

appearance / əˈpɪərəns / n. 外貌，出现

Useful Sentences

1. I'm sorry to hear that.
   听到那个消息我很遗憾。
2. Can you tell me the time and direction of that train?
   能告诉我那趟列车的时间和方向吗?
3. The train has just pulled out of the station. It's bound for Lin Ping.
   列车刚刚驶出车站,它是开往临平的。
4. Could you please describe your handbag as detailedly as possible?
   您能尽可能详细地描述一下您的手提包吗?
5. Please tell me when you lost your luggage and what items were in it.
   请告诉我遗失行李箱的时间及行李箱内的物品。
6. Could you please show me your identity card or passport?
   请出示您的身份证或者护照,好吗?
7. When did you notice that your ID card was lost?
   您什么时候发现您的身份证丢了?
8. I'll call the relevant department to check if they've found an ID card.
   我会联系有关部门,看看是否有人捡到身份证。
9. Can you write down his name, age, appearance, and your name? I can look for him through the radio system.
   您能写一下您孩子的姓名、年龄、外貌特征和您的名字吗? 我可以通过广播找他。
10. Let's wait for the good news.
    让我们等待好消息吧。

III. Exercises

Task 1: Fill in the blanks with the words or phrases given in the box. Change the form if necessary.

| exactly | fill out | claim | appearance | be bound for |
| relevant | diploma | turn in | the moment | pull out of |

1. It took me quite a while to _____ the questionnaire.
2. Do you have the _____ experience?
3. I know _____ how she felt.
4. _____ I closed my eyes, I fell asleep.
5. You must _____ your pass when you leave the building.
6. She worked hard to earn her music _____.
7. The ship _____ England.
8. The train began to _____ the station — then suddenly shuddered to a halt.

9. A lot of lost property _____.
10. She had never been greatly concerned about her _____.

Task 2: Fill in the blanks according to the Chinese given in the brackets. Then act the dialogue out with your partner. (P: Foreign Passenger　　M: Metro Employee)

Dialogue A: A foreign passenger has dropped his iPhone into the tracks and he is seeking help from a metro employee.

P: Sorry, 1. _____ (我刚刚把苹果手机掉到轨道上). What should I do?

E: Can you describe your cell phone?

P: Yes, it is a white iPhone 6s 2. _____ (装在一个塑料透明保护套里).

E: Well, if you are in a hurry, please 3. _____ (留下电话号码, 约定时间来取). If you have time, you can wait for it here. 4. _____ (我们将在行车间隔取回您的手机)). Usually, if the train 5. _____ (用第三轨供电), for the safety, we will retrieve your goods 6. _____ (仅在运营结束后). Please deal with it according to the situation.

P: All right. 7. _____ (我急于上班), my name is Alan. I'll give you my phone number. Please give me a call if you find my iPhone. I will come to take it after work.

E: Sure.

P: Well, thank you very much!

E: You are welcome.

Dialogue B: A foreign passenger lost his umbrella on the train. He is asking help from an employee.

E: May I help you?

P: I lost my umbrella. I left it on the train.

E: Don't worry. Would you like to tell me 8. _____ (那趟车的时间和方向吗)?

P: Well, the train just left the station a minute ago.

E: Oh, 9. _____ (你能描述一下你的伞吗)?

P: It's a blue folding umbrella with lace.

E: Well, we will try to find it. Please tell me your name and phone number. 10. _____ (我们一找到, 我就会与您联系).

P: Thank you.

Task 3: Do a role play according to the following situations.

1. A foreigner lost his keys at the East Railway Station on Line 2 around 2:00 p.m. this afternoon. Suppose you are a metro employee. Now he is asking you for help.

2. Suppose you are an employee at the Customer Service Center. Now a foreigner is claiming the missing phone here.

3. A foreigner lost his passport at the metro station. He was worrying about it. Suppose you are a metro employee. Please help him.

Task 4: Translate the following sentences into English.

1. 我的雨伞落在列车上了，怎么办？
2. 列车经过时不能捡手机。请先留下电话号码，稍后联络您。
3. 请告诉我您乘坐的列车时间和方向。
4. 能告诉我您的名字和电话号码吗？我们一找到，我就会与您联系。
5. 天哪！我的手机从站台上掉下去了。

IV. Self-evaluation

	Excellent	Good	Average	Pass	Fail
make conversations with phrases					
participate in pair work and role play					
improve speaking skills					
finish homework independently					
learn the lessons consciously					

Lesson 12 Dealing with Emergency

I. Warming-up

Task 1: Work in pairs to translate the following words and phrases about subway devices or some causes of subway breakdowns into Chinese.

1. fire alarm
2. emergency exit
3. intercom
4. emergency hammer
5. emergency train stop button
6. emergency unlock device
7. emergency door handle
8. fire extinguisher
9. emergency call
10. fire telephone jack
11. emergency brake
12. signal failure
13. power failure
14. failure of the brake system
15. escalator malfunction

Task 2: As a metro employee, what will you do if there is a fire in the subway station?

II. Situational Dialogues

Dialogue 1

Situation: A train operator asks the passengers in the subway car about the emergency braking event. (P: Passenger   T: Train Operator)

T: Who pulled the emergency brake just now?

P: It's me. We need help. My grandpa had a heart attack. I didn't know whom I could turn to for help, so I pulled the emergency brake.

T: Pulling the emergency brake will make the metro train be forced to stop between the stations and the train cannot run. It is helpless to your grandfather's condition. In this case, you should press emergency intercom to talk with me.

P: Well, I don't know. My subconscious reaction is to pull the emergency brake for help.

T: How is your Grandpa?

P: We need a doctor. My grandfather didn't bring Kyushin pills.

T: OK, I will report it to the general traffic controller. Please dial 120 to let the ambulance wait at the next station. I'll have to reset the emergency braking system immediately so that the train can continue to run. It will take 2 minutes to arrive at the next stop.

P: OK.

T: Please keep in mind next time that only in the following case—a passenger is caught by the door or dragged by trains—should you pull the emergency brake to force the train to stop to save people's lives. You are expected not to pull the emergency brake in case of fire, crime and sudden sick passengers in the cars, since it will force the train to stop between two stations and thus delay the rescue.

P: Yes, thank you!

对话1

情景：列车司机向车厢里的乘客询问列车被紧急制动事件。(P为乘客   T为列车司机)

T: 刚才谁拉下了紧急制动装置？

P: 是我，我们需要帮助。我爷爷突发心脏病。我不知道求助谁，所以才拉了紧急制动。

T: 拉了紧急制动会让列车被迫停在区间动不了，对您爷爷的病情没有帮助，发生这种情况您按紧急对讲机和我通话就可以了。

P: 哦，我不知道，下意识反应就是拉下紧急制动求救了。

T: 你爷爷情况如何？

P: 我们需要医生，我爷爷没带救心丸。

T: 好的，我向总调度员汇报这一情况。请你拨打120，让救护车等在下一站，我马上重置紧急制动系统，这样列车才能继续运行。运行到下一站需要2分钟。

P: 好的。

T：下次请记住，只有在乘客被车门夹住或者被列车拖行的情况下才能拉紧急制动拉手，让列车停下挽救生命。如果车厢发生火灾、犯罪事件或者突发疾病等情况，你不应该拉下紧急制动拉手，因为这会迫使列车停在两站之间而延误救援。

P：明白了，谢谢！

Dialogue 2

Situation：There is an emergency at the station, which requires evacuation of passengers. (P：Passenger   E：Metro Employee)

P：What happened? Why is everyone so scared?

E：There is an emergency at the station. Please follow the instructions of the staff and leave the station as soon as possible.

P：Can I refund the ticket? How to refund?

E：You can get the refund of a single journey ticket within 7 days at any station or replace your stored-value card free of charge at the Customer Service Center on your next ride.

E：I'm sorry for the inconvenience this might cause. Please leave the station at once.

对话2

情景：车站发生紧急事件，需要疏散乘客。(P为乘客   E为地铁工作人员)

P：发生什么事情了？为什么大家都那么惊慌？

E：现在车站发生了紧急事件，请您听从工作人员的指引，尽快离开车站。

P：车票能退吗？怎么退？

E：您所持的单程票可在7日内在任何车站办理退款手续，储值票可以在下次乘车时去客服中心免费更新。

E：给您带来不便，非常抱歉！请马上出站。

Dialogue 3

Situation：The fire occurred between the two stations, which required emergency evacuation of passengers. (P：Passenger   E：Metro Employee)

P：What should we do? Where should we go?

E：Don't be afraid. You can walk to the train's last car, where the staff will transfer you to the safe area. Please follow the instructions of the staff and evacuate in order.

P：Where are we going to be evacuated?

E：You will be evacuated to the nearest station from here. Our staff will take you there. Please follow the instructions.

E：I'm sorry for the inconvenience this might cause.

对话3

情景：列车在区间内发生火灾，需要紧急疏散乘客。(P为乘客   E为地铁工作人员)

P：我们怎么办？该往哪里走？

E：别害怕，你们可以走到列车最后一节车厢，那里的工作人员会将你们转移到安全区域。请听从我们工作人员的指挥，有序疏散。

P：我们将被疏散到哪里？

E：疏散到离这里最近的车站，工作人员会指引大家过去，请听从指挥。

E：给大家造成不便，非常抱歉！

Dialogue 4

Situation：There is an emergency at the station. The metro company requires the passengers to transfer to buses to their destinations. (P：Passenger   E：Metro Employee)

E：Sorry, there is an emergency at the station. Can you follow the instructions of the staff and take the shuttle bus to your destination?

P：What can I do with this single journey ticket?

E：You can get the shuttle bus ticket for free by your single journey ticket and then refund your single journey ticket at any station within seven days or replace your stored-value card for free at the Customer Service Center on your next ride.

P：OK, where should I go?

E：Where are you going? Our staff will help you to take the right shuttle bus.

P：I'm going to East Railway station.

E：OK, please follow me. You have to take the shuttle bus on the other side of the ground after changing your ticket.

对话 4

情景：车站发生紧急事件，地铁公司启动公交接驳。（P 为乘客   E 为地铁工作人员）

E：打扰一下，车站发生了紧急事件。您能根据工作人员的指引乘坐公交接驳车前往目的地站吗？

P：我怎么处理单程票？

E：您可以凭您的单程票免费获得接驳车票，您的单程票可在 7 日内在任何车站办理退款手续，储值票可以在下次乘车时去客服中心免费更新。

P：好的，我该往哪里走？

E：你要去哪里？工作人员会指引你到相应的地方乘车。

P：我要去火车东站。

E：好的，请跟我走，你要乘坐的接驳车需要换票后到另外一边的地面接驳站台乘车。

Words and Phrases

train operator：列车司机

emergency brake：紧急制动装置

intercom / ˈɪntəkɒm / n. 对讲机

subconscious / ˌsʌbˈkɒnʃəs / a. 潜意识的，下意识的

general traffic controller：总调度员

reset / ˌriːˈset / v. 重置，重新设定
drag / dræg / v. 拖，拉，拽
in case of：如果发生，假如
rescue / ˈreskjuː / v. 营救，援救
evacuation / ɪˌvækjuˈeɪʃn / n. 疏散，撤离
scared / skeəd / a. 害怕的
transfer / trænsˈfəː(r) / v. 转乘，转移
evacuate / ɪˈvækjueɪt / v. 疏散，撤离
in order：秩序井然，按顺序
shuttle bus：接驳车，班车

Useful Sentences

1. Pulling the emergency brake will make the metro train be forced to stop between the stations and the train cannot run.
   拉了紧急制动，会让列车被迫停在区间动不了。

2. Please dial 120 to let the ambulance wait at the next station.
   请你拨打120，让救护车等在下一站。

3. I'll have to reset the emergency braking system immediately so that the train can continue to run.
   我马上重置紧急制动系统，这样列车才能继续运行。

4. You are expected not to pull the emergency brake in case of fire, crime and sudden sick passengers in the cars, since it will force the train to stop between two stations and thus delay the rescue.
   如果车厢发生火灾、犯罪事件或者突发疾病等情况，您不应该拉下紧急制动拉手，因为这会迫使列车停在两站之间而延误救援。

5. You can get the refund of a single journey ticket within 7 days at any station or replace your stored-value card free of charge at the Customer Service Center on your next ride.
   您的单程票可在7日内在任何车站办理退款手续，储值票可以在下次乘车时去客服中心免费更新。

6. You can walk to the train's last car, where the staff will transfer you to the safe area.
   你们可以走到列车最后一节车厢，那里的工作人员会将你们转移到安全区域。

7. Please follow the instructions of the staff and evacuate in order.
   请听从我们工作人员的指挥，有序疏散。

8. You have to take the shuttle bus on the other side of the ground platform after changing your ticket.
   你要乘坐的接驳车需要换票后到另外一边的地面接驳站台乘车。

III. Exercises

Task 1：Fill in the blanks with the words or phrases given in the box. Change the form if necessary.

| subconscious | evacuate | transfer | reset | rescue |
| appropriate | in case of | scared | in order | drag |

1. The patient _____ to another hospital.
2. She is _____ of going out alone.
3. He was as busy as a bee trying to put the house _____.
4. You need to _____ your watch to local time.
5. _____ fire, ring the alarm bell.
6. I _____ the chair over to the window.
7. Many advertisements work at a _____ level.
8. Now that the problem has been identified, _____ action can be taken.
9. Families _____ to safer parts of the city.
10. The bank _____ the company from bankruptcy.

Task 2: Fill in the blanks according to the Chinese given in the brackets. Then act the dialogue out with your partner. (P: Foreign Passenger   E: Metro Employee)

Dialogue A: The train of Line 4 adjusts operation route for some reasons, so all the passengers are asked to get off the train and follow the instructions of the staff.

P: What happened? I didn't hear the broadcasting just now. Will the train of Line 4 still operate?

E: I'm sorry, the operating route of the train of Line 4 1._____ (因某些原因需要被调整). Please 2._____ (听从指导) of the station staff. You can also 3._____ (关注车站广播). I'm sorry for the inconvenience this might cause.

P: Where should I go now? Can I 4._____ (退票)? How to refund?

E: You can go with me. You can also get the refund of a single journey ticket within 7 days at any station or replace your stored-value card free of charge at the Customer Service Center 5._____ (在下次乘车时).

E: Thank you for your cooperation.

Dialogue B: There is a fire at the station, which requires emergency evacuation of passengers.

P: 6._____ (站台着火了)! Hurry up and put out fire!

E: Excuse me, where is the fire?

P: Over there, 7._____ (有很多浓烟).

E: We will put out it immediately. 8._____ (请马上到站厅).

E: The fire is too large. We need to 9._____ (把乘客疏散到车站外), and fire fighters will arrive soon. Please follow the instructions of the staff and 10._____ (立即出站). Thank you for your cooperation.

P: OK, I'll leave right now.

Task 3: Do a role play according to the following situations.

1. The metro train will be 20 minutes late due to the signal failure. A foreigner is very anxious because he will be late for the work if the train delays 20 minutes. Suppose you are a metro employee, you advise him to take the bus or other means of transport.
2. There is a fire in the station suddenly, which causes the power failure. The passengers are very scared. Suppose you are a metro employee, you tell the passengers to remain calm and follow the instructions of the staff to leave the station quickly.
3. There is an emergency in a running train, all the passengers are required to get off the train. Suppose you are a metro employee, you should give evacuation instructions to passengers and ask them to transfer to another train.
4. There is an emergency in a running train, all the passengers have to get off the train. But a foreigner buys a ticket and prepares to go down the platform. Suppose you are a metro employee, you stop him and explain the reason and tell him how to return a ticket.

Task 4: Translate the following sentences into English.

1. 请注意，由于发生紧急情况，我们现在需要清客。
2. 不要惊慌，按照站务员的指示尽快离开车站。
3. 你可以到售票处办理退票。
4. 怎么回事？那边怎么冒浓烟了？
5. 请大家到站台中间去，在疏散标志指引下出站。

IV. Self-evaluation

	Excellent	Good	Average	Pass	Fail
make conversations with phrases					
participate in pair work and role play					
improve speaking skills					
finish homework independently					
learn the lessons consciously					

Lesson 13 Operating in Adverse Weather

I. Warming-up

Task 1: Work in pairs to write out the English words or phrases about adverse climate according to given Chinese.

1. 暴风雨
2. 暴风雪
3. 强降雨
4. 沙尘暴

5. 大雪

6. 大雾

7. 飓风

8. 台风

9. 冰雹

10. 雷暴雨

11. 闪电

12. 冰冻

Task 2: Many people are rushing into the subway station to take shelter from the heavy rain, which makes the station crowded and noisy. Suppose you are a metro employee, how do you deal with this situation?

II. Situational Dialogues

Dialogue 1

Situation: Some passengers are trapped in the subway station due to the rainstorm. A passenger is talking about subway service in the rainstorm with a metro employee. (P: Passenger E: Metro Employee)

E: I'm sorry, but don't crowd at the exit. Please leave a passage for other passengers. The floor is too wet and we are going to spread a non-slip mat here to prevent passengers from falling down on the floor.

P: It is pouring now. We don't take umbrellas, and we can't go until the rain stops.

E: We have distributed a limited number of disposable raincoats at the station. Those who don't get the raincoats, please don't stand at the exit next to elevators. Thank you for your cooperation.

P: Will the rainstorm affect the normal operation of trains?

E: Usually it won't. All trains are in normal service at present. But please be careful about the wet and slippery floor when walking.

P: OK, thank you!

对话1

情景：乘客因暴雨被困在地铁站，一名乘客正和地铁工作人员谈论暴雨天气中的地铁服务。（P为乘客　　E为地铁工作人员）

E：对不起，请大家不要挤在出口。请各位留出通道让乘客通行。地面很湿，我们要铺防滑垫以防乘客在地板上摔倒。

P：现在外面倾盆大雨，我们没有带伞，要等雨停了才能走。

E：我们车站派发了一次性雨衣，但数量有限。没有领到雨衣的乘客请尽量不要站到靠近电梯的出口处，谢谢配合。

P：暴雨会影响列车的正常运营吗？

E：一般不会。目前列车运行一切正常。但是大家走路小心，地面湿滑。

P：好的，谢谢！

Dialogue 2

Situation：The elevated stations are closed and trains are out of service due to the typhoon. A passenger is talking about it with a metro employee. （P：Passenger E：Metro Employee）

P：Is the train running today?

E：No. Affected by typhoon, all elevated stations in different lines will stop operating for the passengers' safety. Trains will run at every ten minutes in the underground stations. When the elevated railways return to normal operating depends on weather conditions. Please pay attention to the station announcement, the official microblog or WeChat, etc.

P：Yes, I see.

E：I'm sorry for the inconvenience this might cause.

P：It's OK.

E：Thank you for your understanding.

对话2

情景：地铁工作人员和乘客谈论因台风造成高架车站关闭和列车停运。（P为乘客 E为地铁工作人员）

P：今天列车运行吗？

E：不运行。受台风的影响，为了您的安全，各条线路的高架车站均停运。在地下车站列车每隔10分钟运行。高架何时恢复正常运营视天气情况而定。请留意车站公告、官方微博、微信等。

P：好的，我知道了。

E：非常抱歉，给您带来不便。

P：没关系。

E：谢谢理解。

Words and Phrases

passage / ˈpæsɪdʒ / *n.* 通道，走廊

non-slip / ˌnɒn ˈslɪp / *a.* 防滑的

mat / mæt / *n.* 垫子

distribute / dɪˈstrɪbjuːt / *v.* 分发

disposable / dɪˈspəʊzəbl / *a.* 一次性的，可任意处理的

in service：在运行，在使用

out of service：停止运行，退职

typhoon / taɪˈfuːn / *n.* 台风

elevated railway：高架铁路

Useful Sentences

1. The floor is too wet and we are going to spread a non-slip mat here to prevent passengers from falling down on the floor.
   地面很湿，我们要铺防滑垫以防乘客在地板上摔倒。
2. We have distributed a limited number of disposable raincoats at the station.
   我们车站派发了一次性雨衣，但数量有限。
3. Will the rainstorm affect the normal operation of trains?
   暴雨会影响列车的正常运营吗?
4. All trains are in normal service at present.
   目前列车运行一切正常。
5. Trains will run at every ten minutes in the underground stations.
   在地下车站列车每隔10分钟运行。
6. When the elevated railways return to normal operating depends on weather conditions.
   高架何时恢复正常运营视天气情况而定。

III. Exercises

Task 1: Fill in the blanks with the words or phrases given in the box. Change the form if necessary.

passage	disposable	in service	mat	out of service	distribute

1. The money _____ among schools in the area.
2. Rail and subway service stopped after the quake, and several lines are still not yet back _____.
3. A dark narrow _____ led to the main hall.
4. Sorry, the number you dial is _____.
5. Wipe your feet on the _____ before you come in, please.
6. It is more hygienic to use _____ paper tissues.

Task 2: Fill in the blanks according to the Chinese given in the brackets. Then act the dialogue out with your partner. (P: Passenger   E: Metro Employee)

Situation: A passenger is talking about subway service in the increment weather with a metro employee. (P: Passenger   E: Metro Employee)

E: Please 1. _____ (注意脚下安全), the road is 2. _____ (又湿又滑). Please take good care of your children. 3. _____ (为了保持车站秩序), please 4. _____ (不要滞留在出口).

P: Yes, I see. I don't take an umbrella.

E: You can go to the Customer Service Center to see 5. _____ (是否有便民伞).

P: OK, thank you.

E: You are welcome!

Task 3: Do a role play according to the following situations.

1. Talk about the subway operation in the heavy fog with a passenger.
2. The metro trains are out of service due to the typhoon. Suppose you are a metro employee, a passenger is talking with you about the subway service in typhoon weather.

Task 4: Translate the following sentences into English.

1. 走路小心，地板又湿又滑。
2. 你需要水和清凉油吗？它们能缓解你的症状。
3. 由于台风，地铁列车停运。
4. 我们将尽力确保列车在暴雨天气的正常运行。

IV. Self-evaluation

	Excellent	Good	Average	Pass	Fail
make conversations with phrases					
participate in pair work and role play					
improve speaking skills					
finish homework independently					
learn the lessons consciously					

Unit 5

Customer Service for Big Events

Learning Objectives

In this unit, you will learn:
- useful words and phrases related to greetings and inquiring during big events;
- how to introduce the time arrangement of the first and last train;
- useful words and phrases related to public service;
- how to introduce your hometown to foreigners.

Lesson 14   Greetings and Inquiring

I. Warming-up

Task 1: Work in pairs. Match the following logos with the correct event names.

a. Beijing Summer Olympics	b. London Summer Olympics
c. Atalanta Summer Olympics	d. Beijing Winter Olympics
e. Hangzhou Asian Games	f. Russia FIFA World Cup

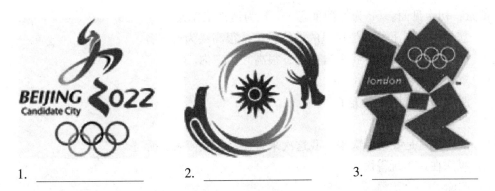

1. _____   2. _____   3. _____

4. _____   5. _____   6. _____

Task 2: How do you usually greet others?

Task 3: Try to use three different languages to greet others.

II. Situational Dialogues

Dialogue 1

Situation: Meeting people for the first time. (P: Foreign Passenger   E: Metro Employee)

E: Hello, my name is Wang Ping. I'm a member of the metro staff here, and I'm glad to help you.

P: Hi, I'm Adam from the USA. Glad to meet you.

E: Welcome to Hangzhou.

P: Thank you. This city is very beautiful.

E: Have you been here before?

P: No, it's my first time here. I'm here to watch a game and, by the way, to have a look around.

E: Have a good stay here!

P: Thanks.

对话1

情景：初次见面。(P 为外国乘客   E 为地铁工作人员)

E：您好，我叫王萍，是这里的地铁员工，很高兴为您服务。

P：你好，我叫艾顿，我来自美国，很高兴认识你。

E：欢迎您来杭州。

P：谢谢，这个城市太美了。

E：之前来过这里吗？

P：没有，这是我第一次来。我这次来看比赛，顺便来旅游。

E：祝您在这里玩得愉快。

P：谢谢。

Dialogue 2

Situation: Talking about the transportation. (P: Foreign Passenger   E: Metro Employee)

E：Is it the first time you have been here?

P：Yes. How is the traffic here? It is said to be terrible.

E：It's convenient to take either subway or buses. However, the roads will be very crowded during rush hours. You can take subway instead during that period.

P：Thank you very much.

对话2

情景：聊交通。（P为外国乘客　　E为地铁工作人员）

E：您是第一次来这里吗?

P：是啊，这里的交通如何？听说很拥堵？

E：坐地铁、公交车都很方便。上下班高峰期路上很拥堵，可以选乘地铁。

P：好的，非常感谢!

Dialogue 3

Situation：Waving goodbye. （P：Foreign Passenger　　E：Metro Employee）

P：Hi, I'm going home this afternoon.

E：Have a good journey, Eason. Welcome back here again.

P：Yes, I will. The metro here is convenient, and the city is beautiful, too. I'll bring my family here next time.

E：Looking forward to seeing you again. Byebye!

P：Bye!

对话3

情景：告别。（P为外国乘客　　E为地铁工作人员）

P：嗨，我今天下午要回家了。

E：伊森，旅途愉快。欢迎您再回来。

P：我会的，你们的地铁很方便，城市也很美。下次我要带我的家人一起过来。

E：期待下次再见到您，再见!

P：再见。

Dialogue 4

Situation：The passenger is going to the West Lake. （P：Foreign Passenger　　E：Metro Employee）

P：Excuse me, what is the most famous scenic spot here?

E：The West Lake is one of the most famous scenic spots in China. Lots of visitors come to this city for the lake.

P：Then how can I get there by metro?

E：You can take Line 1 to the Longxiangqiao Station. It's very convenient.

P：OK. Thank you! Are there any other places to go?

E: A lot! For example, Lingyin Temple is beside the West Lake. Some beautiful ancient legends took place there. And there is also a 5A scenic spot named Xixi Wetland. You should be impressed by the beautiful view.

P: Great! I'll go and see! Thank you.

对话4

情景：乘客打算去西湖。（P 为外国乘客　　E 为地铁工作人员）

P：您好，请问这里最有名的景点是什么？

E：西湖是全国闻名的景点，很多人都会慕名而来。

P：您能告诉我坐地铁怎么去吗？

E：您可以坐1号线在龙翔桥站下车。非常方便。

P：好的，谢谢。请问还有其他推荐的景点吗？

E：景点非常多，比如，灵隐寺就在西湖附近，那里有很多古老美丽的传说。还有国家5A级风景区西溪湿地，风景很美，一定会给你留下深刻印象的。

P：实在是太棒了，我要去看看。谢谢。

Words and Phrases

transportation / ˌtrænspɔːˈteɪʃn / *n.* 交通工具

traffic / ˈtræfɪk / *n.* 交通，运输

it is said to be：据说是……

convenient / kənˈviːniənt / *a.* 方便的

period / ˈpɪəriəd / *n.* 期间

look forward to：盼望，期待

scenic spot：风景区，景点

ancient / ˈeɪnʃənt / *a.* 古老的，古代的

legend / ˈledʒənd / *n.* 传说，传奇

take place：发生

wetland / ˈwetlənd / *n.* 湿地

be impressed by：对……印象深刻

Useful Sentences

1. Have a good stay here!
   祝您在这里玩得愉快。

2. Is it the first time you have been here?
   您是第一次来这里吗？

3. However, the roads will be very crowded during rush hours. You can take subway instead during that period.
   然而，上下班高峰期路上很拥堵，可以选乘地铁。

4. Have a good journey.

   旅途愉快。

5. The West Lake is one of the most famous scenic spots in China. Lots of visitors come to this city for the lake.

   西湖是全国闻名的景点，很多人都会慕名而来。

6. For example, Lingyin Temple is beside the West Lake. Some beautiful ancient legends took place there.

   比如，灵隐寺就在西湖附近，那里有很多古老美丽的传说。

III. Exercises

Task 1: Fill in the blanks with the words given in the box. Change the form if necessary.

transportation	traffic	it is said to be	legend
wetland	be impressed by		

1. She is writing a thesis on Irish _____ and mythology（神话）.
2. Bicycles are a cheap and efficient means of _____.
3. _____ the city's largest ever cultural relics repaired project.
4. I think people would _____ your language abilities.
5. The _____ plays a crucial（重要的）role in producing oxygen and purifying the air.
6. There was heavy _____ on the roads this morning.

Task 2: Imagine you are a metro employee. You meet a foreign visitor at the metro station. Fill in the blanks according to the Chinese version provided in the brackets. Then act the dialogue out with your partner. （P: Foreign Passenger   E: Metro Employee）

P: Good morning, sir. 1. _____（您能帮我个忙吗）?

E: Sure. My name is Wang Ming. 2. _____（我是这个地铁站的工作人员）. I'm glad to help you.

P: Hey, Wang Ming. My name is Sam. I come here for vacation. 3. _____（您知道我能在哪里找到宾馆吗）?

E: What kinds of hotel are you looking for? Budget hotel or luxury hotel?

P: 4. _____（我更喜欢豪华的）. It will be perfect if the hotel is close to the West Lake.

E: Well, there is a Hyatt Hotel beside the West Lake. You can enjoy the beautiful scenery just through the window in your room.

P: Sounds great! How can I get there?

E: You can take Line 1 to Longxiangqiao Station. 5. _____（你一出地铁站就能看见宾馆）.

P: Thank you so much!

E: You're welcome. 6. ＿＿＿＿＿＿＿＿（旅途愉快）.

Task 3: Do a role play according to the following situations.

1. A foreign passenger is asking you the way to a hospital.
2. A foreign passenger is asking you the way to the airport.
3. A foreign passenger is asking you the way to a famous shopping center.
4. Meet a foreign passenger at the metro station and introduce him some scenic spots in Shanghai.

Task 4: Translate the following sentences into English.

1. 欢迎您来杭州。很高兴遇见你。
2. 我在找洗手间，您能告诉我它在哪儿吗？
3. 当然了。事实上，最近的一个就在那边。
4. 乘坐地铁非常方便。
5. 祝您有一个安全的旅途。
6. 您可以乘坐地铁一号线到火车东站。

IV. Self-evaluation

	Excellent	Good	Average	Pass	Fail
make conversations with phrases					
participate in pair work and role play					
improve speaking skills					
finish homework independently					
learn the lessons consciously					

Lesson 15   The First and Last Train

I. Warming-up

Task1: Match the following times with their corresponding English translations.

( ) 1. 11:30   a. eleven-o-five
( ) 2. 6:00   b. eleven thirty
( ) 3. 8:35   c. a quarter past seven
( ) 4. 7:15   d. six o'clock
( ) 5. 11:05   e. twenty-five to nine

Task 2: Have you ever helped others to transfer to metro? If you have, please share your experience with us.

Task 3: What time do you usually take metro?

II. Situational Dialogues

Dialogue 1

Situation: Asking about the first and last train. (P: Foreign Passenger   E: Metro Employee)

P: Excuse me, when does the first train arrive in this station?
E: The first train arrives at 5:30 a.m.
P: When is the last train?
E: 10:30 p.m.

对话 1

情景：询问首末班车。(P 为外国乘客   E 为地铁工作人员)

P：请问这个站的最早一班车是什么时候？
E：本站第一班是早晨 5 点 30 分。
P：这个站最后一班是几点？
E：晚上 10 点 30 分。

Dialogue 2

Situation: The first and last train after a match. (P: Foreign Passenger   E: Metro Employee)

P: Hello, I wonder if there is a time change for the last train because of the football match tonight.
E: Yes, we have got a notice from the Operating Center. The last train will arrive at 11:30 p.m.
P: Thanks!

对话 2

情景：赛事后的首末班车。(P 为外国乘客   E 为地铁工作人员)

P：您好，今天有足球比赛，请问这个站的末班车时间是不是有变化？
E：是的，我们收到运营总部的通知，末班车运营到晚上 11 点 30 分。
P：谢谢！

Dialogue 3

Situation: Asking about the departing interval. (P: Foreign Passenger   E: Metro Employee)

P: Excuse me, what time is the next train?
E: About 3 minutes later.
P: What is the departing interval?
E: In rush-hours, the departing interval is 3 minutes. But in non-rush hours, the interval is 7 minutes.
P: Thank you!

E: It's my pleasure.

对话3

情景：询问发车间隔。（P 为外国乘客   E 为地铁工作人员）

P: 请问下一班车什么时候到？

E: 大概3分钟后。

P: 列车间隔是多少？

E: 在高峰期列车间隔是3分钟，但在平峰期列车间隔是7分钟。

P: 谢谢。

E: 不用客气。

Dialogue 4

Situation: Missing the last train. (P: Foreign Passenger   E: Metro Employee)

P: Excuse me, sir. What time is the next train?

E: Which line do you want to take?

P: Line 1. I'm heading for the Central Park.

E: Sorry, the last train of Line 1 has just departed.

P: Oh, no! What should I do now?

E: Don't worry. You can take Line 3 and transfer to Line 5 at West Street Station. It will take you to the Central Park, too.

P: When is the last train of Line 3 and Line 5?

E: The last train of Line 3 at our station will arrive at 11:00 p.m. and the last train of Line 5 will arrive at 11:45 p.m. You won't miss them.

P: Thank you so much!

E: My pleasure.

对话4

情景：错过末班车。（P 外国乘客   E 为地铁工作人员）

P: 抱歉，先生。请问下一班车什么时候来？

E: 您要坐几号线？

P: 1号线。我要去中央公园。

E: 抱歉，1号线的末班车刚刚开走。

P: 哦，天呐！我该怎么办？

E: 别着急，您可以坐3号线在西街站换乘5号线。它也能带您去中央公园。

P: 3号线和5号线的末班车是什么时候？

E: 3号线在本站的末班车会在晚上11点到站，5号线的末班车会在11点45分到站。你不会错过它们的。

P: 非常感谢！

E：别客气。

Words and Phrases

the first train：首班车

the last train：末班车

wonder /ˈwʌndə(r)/ v. 想知道，疑惑

time change：时间调整

notice /ˈnəʊtɪs/ n. 通知

Operating Center：运营中心

interval /ˈɪntəvl/ n. 间隔，间距

depart /dɪˈpɑːt/ v. 离开

departing interval：发车间隔

Useful Sentences

1. When is the last train?
   末班车是几点？

2. The last train will arrive at 11：30 p. m.
   末班车会在晚上 11 点 30 分到。

3. What is the departing interval?
   列车间隔是多少？

4. In rush-hours, the departing interval is 3 minutes. But in non-rush hours, the interval is 7 minutes.
   在高峰期列车间隔是 3 分钟，但在平峰期列车间隔是 7 分钟。

5. Sorry, the last train of Line 1 has just departed.
   抱歉，1 号线的末班车刚刚开走。

III. Exercises

Task 1：Fill in the blanks with the words given in the box. Change the form if necessary.

the last train	wonder	time change	notice
interval	depart		

1. He's starting to _____ whether he did the right thing in accepting this job.
2. The plane _____ at 6 a. m.
3. The plants should be spaced at six-inch _____.
4. The computer did not resync（重新同步）because the required _____ was too big.
5. I wouldn't like to be tied to catching _____ home.
6. There was a large _____ on the wall saying "No Parking."

Task 2: Imagine you are a metro employee. You meet a foreign passenger at the metro station. Fill in the blanks according to the Chinese version provided in the brackets. Then act the dialogue out with your partner. (P: Foreign Passenger   E: Metro Employee)

P: Excuse me, sir. Would you please do me a favor?

E: 1. _____ (当然可以。怎么了)?

P: I need to go to Wangfujing Station. But I think I have missed the last train of Line 2. 2. _____ (我应该怎么办)?

E: Wait for a moment please. 3. _____ (让我帮您查一查).

P: Thank you.

E: Well, we are at Chegongzhuang Station. 4. _____ (您可以搭乘 4 号线到西单站). And then, transfer to Line 1 to Wangfujing Station.

P: But I remember the last train at Xidan Station departs at 11:00 p.m. 5. _____ (我觉得我可能赶不上车了).

E: The last train used to depart at 11:00 p.m. However, the timetable has been changed last week. The last train will arrive at Xidan Station at 11:30 p.m. You won't miss it.

P: It's great! Thank you so much!

E: You're welcome. 6. _____ (祝您有个安全的旅途).

Task 3: Do a role play according to the following situations.

1. A foreign passenger is asking about the first and last train at your station.
2. A foreign passenger is asking about the departing interval during rush hours.
3. A foreign passenger comes to Beijing to watch the Winter Olympics. Explain the time change for the last train during that period.
4. A foreign passenger has missed the last train. Give him some advice.

Task 4: Translate the following sentences into English.

1. 首班车是几点?
2. 我还需要等多久?
3. 上一辆刚刚开走。
4. 现在是高峰期,每班间隔 3 分钟,所以你不需要等很长时间。
5. 我想我可能错过了 2 号线的末班车。
6. G20 期间这个站的末班车时间是不是有变化?

IV. Self-evaluation

	Excellent	Good	Average	Pass	Fail
make conversations with phrases					
participate in pair work and role play					
improve speaking skills					
finish homework independently					
learn the lessons consciously					

Lesson 16　Public Service

I. Warming-up

Task 1：Match the English words or phrases with their corresponding pictures.

| a. invoice | b. luggage | c. injury | d. run out of battery |

1. _____

2. _____

3. _____

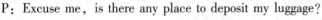
4. _____

Task 2：What will you do if your mobile phone runs out of battery while you are outside?

Task 3：Do you know how to deposit luggage in a subway station?

II. Situational Dialogues

Dialogue 1

Situation：Depositing luggage. (P：Foreign Passenger　　E：Metro Employee)

P：Excuse me, is there any place to deposit my luggage?

E：Sorry. For safety reasons, you can't deposit luggage in a metro station during the G20. I apologize for any inconvenience it may cause.

P：OK. That's fine.

对话1

情景：行李寄存。(P 为外国乘客　　E 为地铁工作人员)

P：请问车站有行李寄存处吗？

E：抱歉。为了安全考虑，G20期间地铁站不能寄存行李。对此可能造成的不便，我深表歉意。

P：好的。没关系。

Dialogue 2

Situation：Accidental injuries. (P：Foreign Passenger　　E：Metro Employee)

P：Excuse me, I twisted my ankle.

E：Don't worry. I'll call the Emergency Center. You should go to the hospital and check if you have also hurt your bone.

P：OK. Thanks! But I wonder whether the doctors in the hospital can speak English. I come here for the international football match. I can't speak Chinese at all.

E：No worries. I think they can speak English. If you don't mind, I'll send you to the lounge on a wheelchair and wait for the ambulance.

P：Thank you so much!

E：It's my duty.

对话2

情景：意外受伤。（P为外国乘客　　E为地铁工作人员）

P：您好，我不小心扭伤脚了！

E：您别着急，我帮您打急救中心的电话，您到医院检查看看是否伤到骨头了。

P：好的，谢谢。但是我不知道医院的医生是否会说英语。我是来参加国际足球赛的。我一点中文都不会说。

E：放心吧，我想他们会说英语的。如果您不介意的话，我用轮椅送您到休息室等待救护车过来。

P：非常感谢。

E：这是我的职责。

Dialogue 3

Situation：Running out of battery. (P：Foreign Passenger　　E：Metro Employee)

P：Excuse me. My phone is out of battery. Can I borrow your phone to call my friend?

E：Sorry, metro staff are not allowed to take phones while working. But maybe you can call your friend at our controlling center. They will help you.

P：Where is the controlling center?

E：Go straight and turn right at the first corner. And then, go up stairs. You will see the controlling center in front of you. The staff there will help you.

P：Thank you.

对话3

情景：手机没电了。（P为外国乘客　　E为地铁工作人员）

P：不好意思，我的手机没有电了，可以借您的电话给我朋友打电话吗？

E：抱歉，地铁工作人员不允许带手机上岗，您可以到我们车站控制中心给您的朋友打个电话。

P：控制中心在哪里？

E：笔直走，第一个拐角处右转，然后上楼，您会看见控制中心就在您的面前。那里的工作人员会帮助您。

P：太谢谢了。

Dialogue 4

Situation：Asking for invoices. （P：Foreign Passenger　　E：Metro Employee）

P：Excuse me, where can I get an invoice?

E：You can ask for an invoice at the Customer Service before you get out of the station. You need to take the ticket with you. Once you get out of the station, you can't ask for it.

P：OK, thank you.

对话 4

情景：换取发票。（P 为外国乘客　　E 为地铁工作人员）

P：请问哪里可以领发票？

E：请您在出站前凭车票到客服中心领取，出站后不允许领取发票。

P：好的，太谢谢了。

Dialogue 5

Situation：Passenger flow control. （P：Foreign Passenger　　E：Metro Employee）

E：Madam, now we are in a flow control since there are too many people in the station. Please follow the directions of our staff.

P：But I'm in a hurry! It's too time consuming!

E：There might be a stampede if too many people rush in the station. Please cooperate for the safety reason.

P：OK.

对话 5

情景：客流量控制。（P 为外国乘客　　E 为地铁工作人员）

E：女士，由于车站乘车人数较多，现在车站启动客流控制预案，请听从车站工作人员的指引乘车。

P：我赶时间，这样太浪费时间了！

E：车站挤满人会造成踩踏事故。为了您和他人的乘车安全，请您配合我们的工作！

P：好吧！

Words and Phrases

deposit / dɪˈpɒzɪt / v. 存放
inconvenience / ˌɪnkənˈviːniəns / n. 不方便
accidental / ˌæksɪˈdentl / a. 意外的
twist / twɪst / v. 扭
Emergency Center：急救中心
bone / bəʊn / n. 骨，骨骼
lounge / laʊndʒ / n. 休息室
wheelchair / ˈwiːltʃeə (r) / n. 轮椅
battery / ˈbætri / n. 电池
be out of：没有
controlling center：控制中心
invoice / ˈɪnvɔɪs / n. 发票
consume / kənˈsjuːm / v. 消耗
stampede / stæmˈpiːd / n. 惊跑

Useful Sentences

1. Excuse me, is there any place to deposit my luggage?
   请问车站有行李寄存处吗？

2. I apologize for any inconvenience it may cause.
   对此可能造成的不便，我深表歉意。

3. I'll call the Emergency Center. You should go to the hospital and check if you have also hurt your bone.
   我帮您打急救中心的电话，您到医院检查看看是否伤到骨头了。

4. I come here for the international football match. I can't speak Chinese at all.
   我是来参加国际足球赛的。我一点中文都不会说。

5. If you don't mind, I'll send you to the lounge on a wheelchair and wait for the ambulance.
   如果您不介意的话，我用轮椅送您到休息室等待救护车过来。

6. Sorry, metro staff are not allowed to take phones while working.
   抱歉，地铁工作人员不允许带手机上岗。

7. You can ask for an invoice at the Customer Service before you get out of the station. You need to take the ticket with you. Once you get out of the station, you can't ask for it.
   请您在出站前凭车票到客服中心领取，出站后不允许领取发票。

III. Exercises

Task 1：Fill in the blanks with the words given in the box. Change the form if necessary.

| deposit | inconvenience | accidental | twist |
| lounge | be out of | | |

1. She slipped on the ice and _____ her knee.
2. I _____ my luggage in a locker at the station.
3. All the family were sitting in the _____ watching television.
4. Having to wait for ten minutes was a minor _____.
5. The site was located after the _____ discovery of bones in a field.
6. He will soon _____ hospital.

Task 2: Imagine you are a metro employee. A foreign passenger is asking for a metro map. Fill in the blanks according to the Chinese version provided in the brackets. Then act the dialogue out with your partner. (P：Foreign Passenger   E：Metro Employee)

P：Excuse me. 1. _____ (我能问您个问题吗)?
E：Sure. 2. _____ (请说).
P：I'm new here. 3. _____ (我不知道我在哪里可以拿到地铁地图).
E：You can get a free map on the brochure cabinets at both the ends of our station. Or you can ask for one at the Customer Service.
P：Thank you!

P：Hello. 4. _____ (您能给我一份地铁地图吗)?
E：Sorry, 5. _____ (我们这里的地图刚刚发完了). Would you wait for a moment? My colleagues will bring new ones soon. 6. _____ (或者您可以去其他站拿).
P：OK, I see. Thank you!

Task 3: Do a role play according to the following situations.
1. A foreign passenger is asking for bicycle depositing.
2. A foreign passenger wants to borrow a mobile phone charger from a metro employee since his phone has been out of battery.
3. A foreign passenger is asking for invoices after he has got out of the station.
4. A foreign passenger with a big suitcase is looking for a lift.

Task 4: Translate the following sentences into English.
1. 我带您过去。
2. 我们要走绿色通道。
3. 抱歉，我们站没有无障碍卫生间，您可以去龙翔桥车站。
4. 为了安全起见，亚运会期间地铁站不能寄存行李。
5. 我在地图上指给您看。
6. 上海所有地铁站轮椅都可以出入。

IV. Self-evaluation

	Excellent	Good	Average	Pass	Fail
make conversations with phrases					
participate in pair work and role play					
improve speaking skills					
finish homework independently					
learn the lessons consciously					

Lesson 17　The Asian Games

I. Warming-up

Task 1: Work in pairs. Match the following scenic spots with their names.

| a. the West Lake | b. Duanqiao | c. Leifeng Pagoda |
| d. Baochu Pagoda | e. Lingyin Temple | f. Xixi National Wetland Park |

1. _____　　2. _____　　3. _____

4. _____　　5. _____　　6. _____

Task 2: Where is the venues of the 2022 Hangzhou Asian Games?

Task 3: What's the mascot of the 2022 Hangzhou Asian Games?

II. Situational Dialogues

Dialogue 1

Situation: The venues of the Asian Games. (P: Foreign Passenger　　E: Metro Employee)

P: Where are the venues of the Asian Games?

E: The main venue of Hangzhou Asian Games is located at Hangzhou Olympic and International Expo Center. Shaped like a lotus, this center consists of an 80,000-seat main stadium and a 10,000-seat tennis court. A great number of low-carbon technics are used in the main venue to support the theme of "Green Asian Games."

P: Thank you very much!

对话1

情景：亚运会场馆。（P为外国乘客　　E为地铁工作人员）

P：这届亚运会在哪里举办？

E：杭州亚运会的主会场在杭州奥体博览城，外形犹如"莲花碗"，由八万座的主体育场和一万座的网球决赛场通过平台相连，主会场采用了大量绿色低碳技术，打造"绿色亚运"的主题。

P：非常感谢！

Dialogue 2

Situation: Introducing Hangzhou. (P: Foreign Passenger　　E: Metro Employee)

P: This is the first time I've been to Hangzhou.

E: Welcome to Hangzhou.

P: Can you give me a brief introduction of this city?

E: Sure. Hangzhou is a well-known tourist destination in China. It is world-famous for the splendid landscape of the West Lake. The old saying "Just as there is paradise in the heaven, there are Hangzhou and Suzhou on the earth" expresses a heartfelt praise to this city through ages. Located at the southern part of the Yangtze River Delta, Hangzhou has four typical seasons. There are a lot of famous scenic spots in this city: like the West Lake, Duanqiao, Leifeng Pagoda, Lingyin Temple, Three Pools Mirroring the Moon, Qiandao Lake, and the Xixi National Wetland Park. You can get to all those places by metro.

P: Thanks a lot!

对话2

情景：介绍杭州。（P为外国乘客　　E为地铁工作人员）

P：这是我第一次来杭州。

E：杭州欢迎您。

P：您能给我简单介绍一下这个城市吗？

E：杭州是中国著名旅游城市，以其美丽的西湖山水著称于世。"上有天堂，下有苏杭"，表达了古往今来人们对这座美丽城市的由衷赞美。杭州地处长江三角洲南沿，四季分明。杭州有很多著名景点，比如西湖、断桥、雷峰塔、灵隐寺、三潭印月、千岛湖、西溪湿地等，这些景区您都可以乘坐地铁到达。

P：非常感谢！

Dialogue 3

Situation：The passenger is going to the Main Hall of the Asian Games. （P：Foreign Passenger   E：Metro Employee）

P：Hello. I'm going to watch the Opening Ceremony in the Main Hall. Which line shall I take?

E：You can take Line 5 to the station of Asian Village.

P：Do I need to change?

E：Yes. You can take metro to the Citizen Center from this station, transfer to Line 5, and you will get to the Main Hall.

P：OK. Thank you.

对话3

情景：乘客打算去亚运主会馆。（P为外国乘客   E为地铁工作人员）

P：您好，我想去亚运主会馆看开幕式，我该如何坐地铁？

E：您可以乘坐5号线到亚运村站下。

P：请问需要换乘吗？

E：需要换乘。您从我们这个站坐到市民中心站下车，换乘5号线到亚运主会场就可以了。

P：好的，谢谢。

Dialogue 4

Situation：A metro employee is persuading a passenger that he should have a drink of his drink due to the security check upgrade. （P：Foreign Passenger   E：Metro Employee）

E：Good morning, sir. I'm sorry that you should have a drink of your water due to the security check upgrade during the Asian Games.

P：But I don't want to drink anything now.

E：For your safety, every passenger should do so. And also, it's our duty. Please cooperate.

P：Fine.

对话4

情景：亚运会安检升级，随身携带的饮料需要开瓶试饮，工作人员正在说服一位乘客配合。（P为外国乘客   E为地铁工作人员）

E：上午好，先生。很抱歉，由于亚运会期间安检升级，您携带的矿泉水需要您开瓶试饮。
P：我现在不想喝水。
E：为了安全起见，每一位乘客都是如此，我们只是履行我们的职责，请您配合。
P：好吧！

Words and Phrases

venue / ˈvenjuː / n. 场馆
the Asian Games：亚运会
symbolize / ˈsɪmbəlaɪz / v. 象征
shaped / ʃeɪpt / a. 成某种形状的
lotus / ˈləʊtəs / n. 莲花
stadium / ˈsteɪdiəm / n. 体育场
low-carbon technics：低碳技术
splendid / ˈsplendɪd / a. 辉煌的，灿烂的
landscape / ˈlændskeɪp / n. 风景
old saying：俗话
paradise / ˈpærədaɪs / n. 天堂
heaven / ˈhevn / n. 天堂，天空
heartfelt / ˈhɑːtfelt / a. 衷心的
through ages：古往今来
Yangtze River Delta：长江三角洲
typical / ˈtɪpɪkl / a. 典型的
Opening Ceremony：开幕式
Asian Village：亚运村
upgrade / ˈʌpɡreɪd / n. 升级

Useful Sentences

1. Shaped like a lotus, this center consists of an 80,000-seat main stadium and a 10,000-seat tennis court.
   外形犹如"莲花碗"，由八万座的主体育场和一万座的网球决赛场通过平台相连。

2. A great number of low-carbon technics are used in the main venue to support the theme of "Green Asian Games."
   主会场采用了大量绿色低碳技术，打造"绿色亚运"的主题。

3. Hangzhou is a well-known tourist destination in China. It is world-famous for the splendid landscape of the West Lake.
   杭州是中国著名旅游城市，以其美丽的西湖山水著称于世。

4. Just as there is paradise in the heaven, there are Hangzhou and Suzhou on the earth.
   上有天堂，下有苏杭。

5. Located at the southern part of the Yangtze River Delta, Hangzhou has four typical seasons.

杭州地处长江三角洲南沿，四季分明。

6. I'm sorry that you should have a drink of your water due to the security check upgrade during the Asian Games.

很抱歉，由于亚运会期间安检升级，您携带的矿泉水需要您开瓶试饮。

III. Exercises

Task 1: Fill in the blanks with the words given in the box. Change the form if necessary.

| upgrade | heaven | splendid | paradise |
| heartfelt | through ages | typical | |

1. The _____ to version 5.0 costs $395.
2. This mall is a shoppers' _____.
3. I must look like the _____ tourist with my shorts and my camera.
4. We had a _____ holiday.
5. Many fairy tales have been coined（杜撰）about the Huangshan Mountain _____, hiding Huangshan in mystery.
6. We stared up at the _____ trying to see the comet（彗星）.
7. Please accept my _____ apologies.

Task 2: Imagine you are a metro employee, and you are introducing the local famous food to a foreign passenger. Fill in the blanks according to the Chinese version provided in the brackets. Then act the dialogue out with your partner. (P: Foreign Passenger E: Metro Employee)

P: Hey, my name is Amy. 1. _____（我是新来这里的）. May I ask you some questions?

E: Sure. 2. _____（我能为您做点什么吗）?

P: 3. _____（这是我第一次来这里）. I come here for the Asian Games, and I want to have some local food. 4. _____（您能给我些建议吗）?

E: Well, Hangzhou is a culinary paradise with a large number of delicious dishes. As a branch of Zhejiang Cuisine（烹饪）, Hangzhou Cuisine is characterized by freshness and sweetness. We have a lot of world-famous dishes, like West Lake Carp in Sweet and Sour Sauce, Dongpo Pork, Beggar's Chicken, Sister Song's Fish Broth, and Shelled Shrimps with Green Tea.

P: 5. _____（听起来棒极了）. Where can I find these local foods?

E: Actually, you can find these delicious foods everywhere in the city. There are many good restaurants near the West Lake. 6. _____（您可以去那边看一看）.

P: 7. _____（我该怎么去那边）?

E: 8. _____（您可以搭乘1号线到湖滨下车）.

P: Thank you very much!

E: You are welcome. Have a nice day!

Task 3: Do a role play according to the following situations.

1. A foreign passenger is asking about the climate in Hangzhou.
2. A foreign passenger is asking about the scenic spots in Hangzhou.
3. A foreign passenger wants to go to the Hangzhou Olympic and International Expo Center to watch the Asian Games. Give him the directions.
4. A foreign passenger is asking about the metro departing interval during the Asian Games.

Task 4: Translate the following sentences into English.

1. 杭州是世界闻名的旅游城市。
2. 杭州亚运会的主场馆在杭州奥体中心。
3. 开幕式当晚地铁将通宵运营。
4. 亚运会期间地铁安检将升级。
5. 亚运会期间，地铁列车间隔是3分钟。

IV. Self-evaluation

	Excellent	Good	Average	Pass	Fail
make conversations with phrases					
participate in pair work and role play					
improve speaking skills					
finish homework independently					
learn the lessons consciously					

Appendix 1
Words and Phrases 单词和短语

Lesson 1 Inquiring and Directing

route / ruːt / n. 路线
transfer stop：换乘站
head for：前往
miss the stop：坐过头了
opposite / ˈɒpəzɪt / a. 相反的
pull in：进站
destination / ˌdestɪˈneɪʃn / n. 目的地，终点

Lesson 2 Complaints and Suggestions

electric / ɪˈlektrɪk / a. 电动的
normal / ˈnɔːml / a. 正常的，常规的
accessibility / əkˌsesəˈbɪləti / n. 易接近
aisle / aɪl / n. 过道，通道
pass through：通过
wheelchair accessible facility：无障碍设施
hotline / ˈhɒtlaɪn / n. 热线
effectively / ɪˈfektɪvli / ad. 有效地
make a complaint：投诉
in charge of：负责，主管
duty station master：值班站长
extend / ɪkˈstend / v. 给予，提供，发出（邀请等）
severely / sɪˈvɪəli / ad. 严重地，严厉地
criticize / ˈkrɪtɪsaɪz / v. 批评
green hand：新手
deploy / dɪˈplɔɪ / v. 配置，部署

Lesson 3 Broadcasting

Broadcasting Room：广播室

failure / ˈfeɪljə (r) / n. 失败，故障
drill / drɪl / n. 训练
fire drill：火警演习
in order：有序地，依次序地

Lesson 4　Buying Tickets and Checking Tickets

Ticket Vending Machine：自动售票机
ticket office：售票处
destination / ˌdestɪˈneɪʃn / n. 目的地
corresponding / ˌkɒrəˈspɒndɪŋ / a. 对应的
coin-return：找零处
Automatic Gate Machine：自动检票机，闸机
magnetic / mæɡˈnetɪk / a. 有磁性的
top up：充值
Add Value Machine：充值机
recharge / ˌriːˈtʃɑːdʒ / v. 充值
Customer Service Center：客服中心
multiple / ˈmʌltɪpl / a. 许多的
stored-value card：储值卡
appropriate / əˈprəʊpriət / a. 适当的
deposit / dɪˈpɒzɪt / n. 押金，存款
confirm / kənˈfɜːm / v. 确认
transfer / trænsˈfɜː (r) / n. 换乘
accumulate / əˈkjuːmjəleɪt / v. 积累
complicated / ˈkɒmplɪkeɪtɪd / a. 复杂的
QR code：二维码
deduct / dɪˈdʌkt / v. 扣除，减去

Lesson 5　Ticket Machine Failure

jam / dʒæm / v. 塞满，卡住
refund / ˈriːfʌnd / n. 退款，偿还
out of service：暂停服务，失效
all the same：仍然，依然
failure / ˈfeɪljə (r) / n. 故障，失败
exchange / ɪksˈtʃeɪndʒ / v. 兑换，交换
reclaim / rɪˈkleɪm / v. 收回，回收
deduct / dɪˈdʌkt / v. 扣除

Lesson 6 Handling Ticket Services in Different Situations

paid area：付费区
departure station：出发站
overtravel / ˈəʊvətrævəl / n. 超程
update / ˌʌpˈdeɪt / v. 更新
overtime / ˈəʊvətaɪm / ad. 超出时间地
refer to：参考
extra / ˈekstrə / a. 额外的
swipe / swaɪp / v. 刷（卡）
non-paid area：非付费区
invalid ticket：无效票
expired ticket：过期票
issue / ˈɪʃuː / v. 发行，发表
magnetism / ˈmæɡnətɪzəm / n. 磁性
magnetization / ˌmæɡnətɪˈzeɪʃən / n. 磁化
non-registered / nɒn ˈredʒɪstəd / a. 不记名的
in accordance with：按照
receipt / rɪˈsiːt / n. 收据

Lesson 7 Security Check

persuade / pəˈsweɪd / v. 说服，劝说
security check：安检
go through：经过，通过
responsibility / rɪˌspɒnsəˈbɪləti / n. 责任，义务
queue up：排队等候
time-consuming / ˈtaɪm kənˈsjuːmɪŋ / a. 耗时的
permit / pəˈmɪt / v. 允许
significant / sɪɡˈnɪfɪkənt / a. 显著的，有意义的
eye-catching position：醒目位置
announce / əˈnaʊns / v. 宣布，播报
personal belongings：个人物品
balloon / bəˈluːn / n. 气球
inflated / ɪnˈfleɪtɪd / a. 充了气的，膨胀的
forbidden / fəˈbɪdn / a. 被禁止的，严禁的
release / rɪˈliːs / v. 释放
contact net：接触网
explode / ɪkˈspləʊd / v. 爆炸
lead to：导致

panic / ˈpænɪk / n. 恐慌
stampede / stæmˈpiːd / n. 惊跑，人群的蜂拥
durian / ˈduəriən / n. 榴莲
smelly / ˈsmeli / a. 有臭味的
be banned：被禁止
cooperative / kəʊˈɒpərətɪv / a. 合作的

Lesson 8　Security Warnings in the Station

escalator / ˈeskəleɪtə (r) / n. 自动扶梯
lift / lɪft / n. 垂直电梯
for your safety：为了您的安全
luggage / ˈlʌɡɪdʒ / n. 行李
smoking zone：吸烟区
cigarette / ˌsɪɡəˈret / n. 香烟
put out：熄灭
chase / tʃeɪs / v. 追赶，追逐
Escalator Emergency Stop Button：扶梯紧急停梯按钮
firefighting / ˈfaɪəfaɪtɪŋ / n. 消防，灭火
circumstance / ˈsɜːkəmstəns / n. 环境，情况
seal / siːl / n. 密封，封条

Lesson 9　Security Warnings on the Platform

photograph / ˈfəʊtəɡrɑːf / v. 拍照
in secret：机密
moreover / mɔːrˈəʊvə (r) / ad. 而且，此外
influence / ˈɪnfluəns / v. 影响
signaling equipment：信号设备
Part Route：小交路
final stop：终点站
additional / əˈdɪʃnl / a. 附加的，额外的
rush hour：交通拥堵时间，高峰期
relieve / rɪˈliːv / v. 减轻
passenger flow：客流量
pressure / ˈpreʃə (r) / n. 压力
attempt to do sth.：尝试做某事

Lesson 10　Helping the Sick, the Injured and the Disabled

dizzy / ˈdɪzi / a. 晕眩的
heat-stroke / ˈhiːtstrəʊk / n. 中暑

sponge / spʌndʒ / v. 用海绵（或湿布）擦洗

cooling ointment：清凉油

hypoglycemia / ˌhaɪpəʊglaɪˈsiːmiə / n. 低血糖症

scene / siːn / n. 现场，场面

relieve / rɪˈliːv / v. 缓解，减轻

at sb.'s service：愿为某人服务

handrail / ˈhændreɪl / n. 扶手

emergency button：紧急按钮

first-aid kit：急救箱

trap / træp / v. 陷入（困境），设圈套

malfunction / ˌmælˈfʌŋkʃn / n. 故障，失灵

lift / lɪft / n. 电梯

barrier free passage：无障碍通道

attach importance to：重视

accessible elevator：无障碍电梯

wheelchair lifting platform：轮椅升降台

accessibility / əkˌsesəˈbɪləti / n. 可接近性，可达性

Lesson 11　Lost and Found

pull out of：离开，驶离

be bound for：开往，准备到……去

rectangular / rekˈtæŋgjələ(r) / a. 矩形的，长方形的

lattice / ˈlætɪs / n. 格子；格状物

purse / pɜːs / n. 钱包

the moment：一……就……

claim / kleɪm / v. 认领，索取

diploma / dɪˈpləʊmə / n. 文凭

identity card：身份证

fill out：填写

turn in：上交

exactly / ɪgˈzæktli / ad. 确切地，完全地

relevant / ˈreləvənt / a. 相关地

appearance / əˈpɪərəns / n. 外貌，出现

Lesson 12　Dealing with Emergency

train operator：列车司机

emergency brake：紧急制动装置

intercom / ˈɪntəkɒm / n. 对讲机

subconscious / ˌsʌbˈkɒnʃəs / a. 潜意识的，下意识的

general traffic controller：总调度员
reset / ˌriːˈset / v. 重置，重新设定
drag / dræg / v. 拖，拉，拽
in case of：如果发生，假如
rescue / ˈreskjuː / v. 营救，援救
evacuation / ɪˌvækjuˈeɪʃn / n. 疏散，撤离
scared / skeəd / a. 害怕的
transfer / trænsˈfəː(r) / v. 转乘，转移
evacuate / ɪˈvækjueɪt / v. 疏散，撤离
in order：秩序井然；按顺序
appropriate / əˈprəʊpriət / a. 适当的
shuttle bus：接驳车，班车

Lesson 13　Operating in Adverse Weather

passage / ˈpæsɪdʒ / n. 通道，走廊
non-slip / ˌnɒn ˈslɪp / a. 防滑的
mat / mæt / n. 垫子
distribute / dɪˈstrɪbjuːt / v. 分发
disposable / dɪˈspəʊzəbl / a. 一次性的，可任意处理的
in service：在运行，在使用
out of service：停止运行，退职
typhoon / taɪˈfuːn / n. 台风
elevated railway：高架铁路

Lesson 14　Greetings and Inquiring

transportation / ˌtrænspɔːˈteɪʃn / n. 交通工具
traffic / ˈtræfɪk / n. 交通，运输
it is said to be：据说是……
convenient / kənˈviːniənt / a. 方便的
period / ˈpɪəriəd / n. 期间
look forward to：盼望，期待
scenic spot：风景区，景点
ancient / ˈeɪnʃənt / a. 古老的，古代的
legend / ˈledʒənd / n. 传说，传奇
take place：发生
wetland / ˈwetlənd / n. 湿地
be impressed by：对……印象深刻

Lesson 15 The First and Last Train

the first train：首班车
the last train：末班车
wonder / ˈwʌndə (r) / v. 想知道，疑惑
time change：时间调整
notice / ˈnəʊtɪs / n. 通知
Operating Center：运营中心
interval / ˈɪntəvl / n. 间隔，间距
depart / dɪˈpɑːt / v. 离开
departing interval：发车间隔

Lesson 16 Public Service

deposit / dɪˈpɒzɪt / v. 存放
inconvenience / ˌɪnkənˈviːniəns / n. 不方便
accidental / ˌæksɪˈdentl / a. 意外的
twist / ˈtwɪst / v. 扭
Emergency Center：急救中心
bone / bəʊn / n. 骨，骨骼
lounge / laʊndʒ / n. 休息室
wheelchair / ˈwiːltʃeə (r) / n. 轮椅
battery / ˈbætri / n. 电池
be out of：没有
controlling center：控制中心
invoice / ˈɪnvɔɪs / n. 发票
consume / kənˈsjuːm / v. 消耗
stampede / stæmˈpiːd / n. 惊跑

Lesson 17 The Asian Games

venue / ˈvenjuː / n. 场馆
the Asian Games：亚运会
symbolize / ˈsɪmbəlaɪz / v. 象征
shaped / ʃeɪpt / a. 成某种形状的
lotus / ˈləʊtəs / n. 莲花
stadium / ˈsteɪdiəm / n. 体育场
low-carbon technics：低碳技术
splendid / ˈsplendɪd / a. 辉煌的，灿烂的
landscape / ˈlændskeɪp / n. 风景
old saying：俗话

paradise / ˈpærədaɪs / n. 天堂
heaven / ˈhevn / n. 天堂，天空
heartfelt / ˈhɑːtfelt / a. 衷心的
through ages：古往今来
Yangtze River Delta：长江三角洲
typical / ˈtɪpɪkl / a. 典型的
Opening Ceremony：开幕式
Asian Village：亚运村
upgrade / ˈʌpɡreɪd / n. 升级

Appendix 2
Subway Broadcasting 地铁广播

Station announcement

1. Welcome to Hangzhou Subway. Have a nice day.
   欢迎乘坐杭州地铁。祝您旅途愉快。
2. Welcome to Metro Line 1, this train is bound for Xianghu.
   欢迎乘坐地铁1号线,本次列车开往湘湖。
3. Please stand away from the platform edge.
   请勿站立在站台边缘。
4. The train bound for Xianghu is arriving. Please stand behind the yellow line.
   开往湘湖方向的列车即将进站,请您站在安全线以内候车。
5. Please mind the gap between the train and the platform.
   请注意列车与站台之间的缝隙。
6. Your attention please. Exit 2 is closed temporarily. You can get out of the station through Exits 1, 3 and 4.
   请注意! 2号出口临时关闭,您可以从1号、3号、4号出口出站。
7. Dear passengers, please swipe your card at the automatic gate to exit the station.
   亲爱的乘客们,请手持车票依次通过闸机验票出站。
8. Your attention please! Crowd Management Plans are now in operation. Please don't stay inside the station. Follow the directions to exit. Thank you!
   请注意:本站正在进行客流控制,请不要在车站内逗留,请按照指示离开本站。谢谢合作。
9. Your attention please! Crowd Management Plans are now in operation. And some of the entry gates are temporarily closed. They will be back in use in about 10 minutes. Please take turns to enter the station and accept our apologies for any inconvenience or delay this might cause.
   请注意:由于现在列车和车站内过于拥挤,本站正在进行客流控制,部分入闸机暂时关闭,10分钟后开启。请您有序进站,不便之处,敬请谅解。
10. Please take care of your children and belongings. Thank you!
    请照顾好您的小孩,保护好随身携带的物品。谢谢合作。

11. Your attention please! Inflammable, explosive or poisonous items are strictly prohibited anywhere in the station. Thank you!

    请注意：严禁携带易燃、易爆、有毒危险品进站，谢谢合作！

12. Take good care of the facilities in the station and train, and it is prohibited to touch the operational facilities without prior approval.

    爱护站内、车内各项设施。未经允许，不得擅自触动行车设备。

13. Please don't smoke, spit and litter in the station or the train so as to keep these places clean.

    保持站内车内卫生，请勿在此吸烟、吐痰、乱扔杂物。

14. Dear Smith from the U. S, please come to the Customer Service Center. Your parents are waiting for you.

    来自美国的史密斯请至客服中心，您的父母在等您。

Onboard announcement

1. This train is bound for Xianghu. The next station is East Railway Station. Please get ready for your arrival.

   本次列车开往湘湖站，下一站是火车东站。下车的乘客请做好准备。

2. We are now at Fengqi station. Transfer here for Line 2.

   凤起路站到了，可在此站换乘2号线。

3. We are now at East Railway Station. Please get ready to exit from the right side when the train's doors and the platform screen doors are fully open.

   火车东站到了，下车的乘客请在列车门和安全门完全打开后，从右侧车门下车。

4. The next station is closed. This train will not stop at the next station.

   下一站关闭，列车将跳站经过。

5. The next station is Xianghu station, the terminus of the line. Please get ready for your arrival and make sure you have all your belongings with you.

   前方是终点站湘湖站，请携带好随身物品准备下车。

6. This is Xianghu station, terminus of the Line 1. Thank you for riding Line 1.

   1号线终点站湘湖站到了，感谢您乘坐1号线。

Last train service broadcasting

1. Your attention please! This train for Xianghu station is the last one. Please board immediately.

   请注意：本次列车是开往湘湖站方向的末班车，请乘客们尽快上车。

2. Your attention please! The last train for Xianghu station has departed.

   请注意：开往湘湖站及沿途各站的末班车已经开出。

3. Your attention please! The last train for Xianghu station has departed. The last train for Xiashajiangbin station will depart at 10：40 p. m.

   请注意：开往湘湖站的末班车已经开出。开往下沙江滨站的末班车，将于晚上10：40由本站开出。

4. Your attention please! Train service for today has ended. Please leave the station as soon as possible. Thank you!

   请注意：今天的列车服务已经终止，请尽快出站，谢谢。

Emergency broadcasting

1. Attention please. The train bound for Xianghu will stop temporarily for certain reasons. Please wait patiently and follow the directions of our staff. Thank you for your cooperation and sorry for the inconvenience this might cause.

   请注意：开往湘湖方向的列车因故需要临时停车。请乘客们耐心等待，听从工作人员指示。不便之处，敬请谅解。

2. Dear passengers, the current train bound for Xianghu will stop for special reasons. All the passengers on the train, please get off immediately, and change to ground transportation vehicles. Sorry for the inconvenience brought to you.

   亲爱的乘客，由于特殊原因，本次开往湘湖方向的列车将停止服务，请所有乘客立即下车，改乘其他地面交通工具。不便之处，敬请原谅。

3. Attention please. The train bound for Xianghu will be delayed for a short time for special reasons. Please wait patiently. Sorry for the inconvenience brought to you.

   请注意：由于特殊原因，开往湘湖方向的列车将稍有延误。请您耐心等候。不便之处，敬请原谅。

4. Attention please. The train bound for Xianghu will be passing without stopping. Please wait patiently for the next train behind the yellow safety line. Thank you for your cooperation.

   请注意：本次开往湘湖方向的列车本站通过不停车，请您在黄色安全线内耐心等候下一趟列车，谢谢合作。

5. Your attention please! This is an emergency! Please leave the station immediately.

   请注意：本站出现紧急情况，请立即离开本站。

6. Your attention please! The station will be closed because of accidents. Please leave immediately. Thank you for your cooperation.

   请注意：现在发生事故，本站即将关闭，所有乘客必须立即离开，谢谢合作。

7. Your attention please! There is a fire in the station. Please follow the directions and leave immediately. Remain calm, don't run!

   请注意：由于本站发生火灾，请按指示立即离开本站。保持冷静，不要奔跑。

Appendix 3
Security Warnings 安全警示

1. Please go through the security check.
   请您配合安检。
2. Please stand firm and hold the handrail.
   请站稳扶好。
3. Please don't destroy the equipment in the station.
   请不要破坏地铁车站设备。
4. Please don't eat and drink in the station.
   请不要在地铁车站内饮食。
5. Smoking is not allowed in the station.
   请不要在地铁车站内吸烟。
6. Pets are not allowed in the station, except guide dogs.
   请不要携带宠物进站,导盲犬除外。
7. Please take care of your belongings.
   请保管好您的行李物品。
8. Please don't take photos in the station.
   请不要在地铁车站内拍照。
9. Balloons are not allowed in the station.
   请不要携带气球进站。
10. Please stand behind the yellow safety line.
    请不要超越黄色安全线。
11. No littering, please.
    请勿乱扔垃圾。
12. Please don't play or run in the station.
    请不要在站内嬉戏打闹。
13. Thank you for your cooperation.
    感谢您的配合。
14. Please don't carry flammable and explosive articles on board.
    请不要携带易燃易爆危险品进站。

15. Please take care of your children.
    请照顾好您的小孩。
16. Please keep clear of the doors.
    请不要倚靠车门。
17. No rushing, please.
    请不要抢上抢下。
18. Open flame is prohibited in the train.
    请不要在车厢内使用明火。
19. Please don't carry oversize objects into the station.
    请不要携带超大物品进站。
20. Please buy luggage tickets for your overweight luggage.
    超重物品需要购买行李票。
21. Please mind the gap between the train and the platform.
    请注意列车与站台的空隙。
22. For safety reasons, please use the lift if you have baggage or bulky items.
    为了安全起见,携带大件物品请选择垂直电梯。
23. Your attention, please! Please follow the staff directions to exit as the exit gates are not working. Single journey tickets should be returned to our staff, while top-up cards should be charged at the Customer Service Center when you travel next time. We apologize for any inconvenience.
    出站的乘客请注意,因出站闸机故障,请听从工作人员的指引,单程票由工作人员回收,储值票请在下次乘车时到客服中心扣除相应的车资,不便之处,敬请谅解。

Appendix 4

Main Scenic Spots in Hangzhou 杭州市主要旅游景点

1. The West Lake: 3 – 6 hours for sightseeing. It is the only existing cultural heritage of Chinese lakes in the World Heritage List.

    西湖：适合游玩 3~6 小时。现今《世界遗产名录》内中国唯一一处湖泊类文化遗产。

2. Lingyin Temple: 2 – 3 hours for sightseeing. With a long history of 1,700 years, Lingyin Temple is the earliest temple in Hangzhou, and it is one of the ten famous ancient Buddhism Temples.

    灵隐寺：适合游玩 2~3 小时。至今已有 1 700 年的历史，为杭州最早名刹，也是中国佛教禅宗十大古刹之一。

3. Qiandao Lake: 1 – 2 days for sightseeing. Qiandao Lake has a splendid view with clean water. It is a good place for relaxation.

    千岛湖：适合游玩 1~2 天，湖水清澈，湖面风光秀美，是个放松的好地方。

4. Leifeng Pagoda: 2 hours for sightseeing. "Leifeng Pagoda in the Sunset" is one of the Ten Views of the West Lake. Rebuilt in 2002, Leifeng Pagoda is now a modern ancient pagoda. Best pictures of the pagoda can be taken from the Long Bridge.

    雷峰塔：适合游玩 2 小时。雷峰夕照为西湖十景之一。2002 年重建后的雷峰塔是现代化的一座古塔，从长桥的角度拍照片特别美。

5. The Song Dynasty Theme Park: 2 – 3 hours for sightseeing. The best part of the theme park is a show called "The Romance of Song Dynasty."

    宋城：适合游玩 2~3 小时。宋城最精彩的莫过于《宋城千古情》的演出。

6. The Xixi National Wetland Park: 1 – 2 days for sightseeing. Covered by rich plants, Xixi Wetland has a quiet environment with fresh air.

    西溪湿地：适合游玩 1~2 天。西溪湿地植被丰富，环境幽静，空气好。

7. The Nine Creeks and Eighteen Gullies: 2 – 3 hours for sightseeing. This is a unique place with quiet environment and fresh air.

    九溪十八涧：适合游玩 2~3 小时。这个景点风景很独特，空气清新，环境清幽。

8. The Broken Bridge: 1 hour for sightseeing. You can see the best Broken Bridge from when you are boating in the West Lake in winter.

    断桥：适合游玩 1 小时。冬天的断桥最美，但在船上看断桥效果更好。

9. Qiantang River: 1 - 2 hours for sightseeing. There is a splendid view of Qiantang Tides, especially in August.

   钱塘江：适合游玩1~2小时。钱塘江潮水很壮观，一般是在八月份。

10. Gu Hill: 2 - 3 hours for sightseeing. You can have an overview of the whole West Lake from the top of the hill.

    孤山：适合游玩2~3小时。爬上孤山可以俯瞰整个西湖景区，美不胜收。

11. Su Causeway: 1 - 2 hours for sightseeing. It's a quiet and romantic place.

    苏堤：适合游玩1~2小时。苏堤很浪漫、很安静。

12. The Six-harmony Pagoda: 2 hours for sightseeing. Seeing from the top of the pagoda, you will enjoy a broad view of Qiantang River.

    六和塔：适合游玩2小时。登六和塔视野广阔，一览钱塘江美景。

Appendix 5
Sports Names 体育项目名称

Olympic Events:

Swimming, Toxophily, Track and Field, Badminton, Boxing, Basketball, Canoeing, Cycling, Equestrian, Fencing, Football, Gymnastics, Rhythmic Gymnastics, Gymnastics Trampoline, Handball, Field Hocky, Judo, Military Pentathlon, Rowing, Sailing, Shooting, Table Tennis, Taekwondo, Tennis, Triathlon, Volleyball, Weight Lifting, Wrestling.

奥运项目：

游泳、射箭、田径、羽毛球、拳击、篮球、皮划艇、自行车、马术、击剑、足球、体操、艺术体操、蹦床、手球、曲棍球、柔道、现代五项、赛艇、帆船、射击、乒乓球、跆拳道、网球、铁人三项、排球、举重、摔跤

Non-Olympic Events:

Baseball, Softball, Bowling, Billiards (Snooker), Cricket, Sport Dance, Squash, Martial Arts, Board Games (Go, Chess), Rattan Ball, Rugby / American Football, Roller Skating, Karate, Golf, Dragon Boat.

非奥运项目：

棒球、垒球、保龄球、台球、板球、体育舞蹈、壁球、武术、棋类（围棋、象棋）、藤球、橄榄球、轮滑、空手道、高尔夫球、龙舟

Appendix 6

Keys 参考答案

Unit 1   Daily Customer Service in Station

Lesson 1   Inquiring and Directing

I. Warming-up

Task 1: Match the words and expressions with the following pictures.

1~4: bcda

III. Exercises

Task 1: Fill in the blanks with the words given in the box. Change the form if necessary.

1. pulls / pulled in
2. route
3. opposite
4. destination
5. head for

Task 2: Imagine you are a metro employee. A foreign passenger is asking for the way to the restroom. Fill in the blanks according to the Chinese version provided in the brackets. Then act the dialogue out with your partner.

1. Is there a restroom here on the platform?
2. near this platform
3. behind the information desk
4. Go straight forward
5. take the lift to the first floor
6. next to the lift

Task 4: Translate the following sentences into English.

1. It's pretty easy to get there.
2. You should get off the train at the next station.
3. I'm sorry to bother you / Excuse me, is this line to the train station?
4. What time will the next train arrive?

5. How long would it take me to get there?

6. You can take Line 7 to Jing'an Temple, and then transfer to Line 2 to Pudong International Airport.

Lesson 2 Complaints and Suggestions

III. Exercises

Task 1: Fill in the blanks with the words given in the box. Change the form if necessary.

1. complaint
2. complaining
3. electric
4. in charge of
5. extend
6. accessibility

Task 2: Imagine you are a metro employee. A passenger is giving suggestions about the seats on the platform. Fill in the blanks according to the Chinese version provided in the brackets. Then act the dialogue out with your partner.

1. Could I talk with someone in charge of the station?
2. How can I help you?
3. on the platform
4. Besides, some of them are broken.
5. passenger flow
6. Within two weeks.
7. Thank you for your explanation.

Task 4: Translate the following sentences into English.

1. I promise a similar thing won't happen again.
2. It is something you should have considered about beforehand!
3. I'm sorry for the inconvenience.
4. I'm sorry about that. We will educate passengers to be more considerate of others on train.
5. I have a complaint to make. / I want to make a complaint.
6. I'll arrange some maintenance staff to fix the ticket vending machine at once.

Lesson 3 Broadcasting

I. Warming-up

Task 1: Match the words and expressions with the following pictures.

1~3: cab

Task 2: Match the English phrases with their corresponding Chinese meanings.

1~5: caebd

III. Exercises

Task 1: Fill in the blanks with the words given in the box. Change the form if necessary.

1. apologize
2. instructions
3. failures
4. in order
5. broadcast
6. drills

Task 2: Fill in the blanks according to the Chinese version provided in the brackets. Then practice the broadcasts out with your partner.

1. Is there anyone who has lost a suitcase?
2. The door of the toilet near the platform
3. I'm sorry for any inconvenience it might cause.
4. The station is on fire.
5. Thank you for your cooperation.

Task 4: Translate the following sentences into English.

1. All passengers, attention please! Pets, except guide dogs, are not allowed in the station.
2. Please mind the gap between the train and the platform.
3. Your attention, please! As the exit gates are not working, please follow staff's directions to exit the station. Single journey tickets should be returned to our staff, while top-up cards should be charged at the Customer Service Center when you travel next time. We apologize for any inconvenience.
4. All passengers, attention please! Because of the huge passenger flow in the station, please take care of your children.
5. Attention please, passengers with over-weight luggage, please go to the Customer Service Center to buy a luggage ticket. Thank you for your cooperation.
6. Dear passengers, please take care of your belongings. Unattended luggage will be removed and destroyed.

Unit 2　Ticket Service

Lesson 4　Buying Tickets and Checking Tickets

I. Warming-up

Task 1: Work in pairs to match the words and phrases in the box with the following pictures.

1~6: AECBDF

III. Exercises

Task 1: Fill in the blanks with the words or phrases given in the box. Change the form if necessary.

1. destination
2. transferred
3. multiple
4. was confirmed
5. magnetic
6. accumulate
7. deposit
8. top up

Task 2: Fill in the blanks according to the Chinese given in the brackets. Then act the dialogue out with your partner.

1. I have no change
2. exchange money at the Customer Service Center
3. how to buy a single journey ticket through the TVM?
4. metro line, your destination and ticket numbers
5. insert the notes or coins into the slot
6. take away your ticket and change
7. get into the platform.
8. Have a nice trip

Task 4: Translate the following sentences into English.

1. Hello, Ticket Vending Machines only accept 5 yuan or 10 yuan or 1 yuan coins. If you don't have any change, please exchange money at the Customer Service Center.
2. Sorry, this Ticket Vending Machine is out of service. Please choose another one to buy tickets.
3. 100 Yuan has been topped up to your card, please confirm the balance.
4. You can take your ticket and change from the coin-return at the bottom of the machine.
5. Our fares are based on the miles you travel.
6. You will get the corresponding discount if using stored-value card.

Lesson 5 Ticket Machine Failure

I. Warming-up

Task 1: Work in pairs to match the English phrases with their corresponding Chinese meanings.

1~5: DEBCF   6~8: AGH

III. Exercises

Task 1: **Fill in the blanks with the words given in the box. Change the form if necessary.**

1. refund
2. reclaim
3. jammed
4. will be deducted
5. exchange

Task 2: **Fill in the blanks according to the Chinese given in the brackets. Then act the dialogue out with your partner.**

1. the Add Value Machine is out of service due to a machine failure.
2. to maintain it
3. top up your card at the Customer Service Center
4. solve your problem soon
5. to keep you waiting for a long time
6. please try it again.

Task 4: **Translate the following sentences into English.**

1. Excuse me, I put my single journey ticket into the slot just now but the gate did not open.
2. Please sign your name in this form and I'll give you a free ticket to get out of the station.
3. This TVM is out of service. Please go to another one to buy a single journey ticket.
4. Maybe there is something wrong with the machine.

Lesson 6　Handling Ticket Services in Different Situations

I. Warming-up

Task 1: **Work in pairs and write down the English words or phrases according to the given Chinese.**

1. E. corresponding fare
2. A. non-registered card
3. L. invalid ticket
4. G. expired ticket
5. F. overtime
6. C. overtravel
7. B. failure
8. H. magnetic card
9. I. ticket conductor
10. K. irregular tickets
11. D. no entry record
12. J. no exit record

III. Exercises

Task 1: Fill in the blanks with the words or phrases given in the box. Change the form if necessary.

1. swipe
2. be registered
3. extra
4. expire
5. refer to
6. to update
7. in accordance with
8. overtime

Task 2: Fill in the blanks according to the Chinese given in the brackets. Then act the dialogue out with your partner.

1. there is an entrance record on it
2. from the time you swiped the card to now
3. reclaim your card
4. Thank you for your cooperation
5. I will deal with it immediately
6. there is no exit information in your last ride
7. which station you came out of last ride
8. you can use it regularly

Task 4: Translate the following sentences into English.

1. Your ticket is overtime, you need to pay the extra fee.
2. There is an entry gate record in your single journey ticket and it has been over 20 minutes till now. The ticket should be reclaimed as required.
3. Your ticket is invalid, please buy it again.
4. Your card has no magnetism, we can change a new card for you.
5. Please fill out your name and phone number on the receipt.

Unit 3 Subway Security

Lesson 7 Security Check

I. Warming-up

Task 1: Work in pairs and look at the following security signs. Discuss them with your partner and match them with the phrases in the box.

1~7: ebgfdac

III. Exercises

Task 1: Fill in the blanks with the words given in the box. Change the form if necessary.

1. persuaded
2. lead to
3. cooperative
4. time-consuming
5. permit
6. Panic
7. release
8. forbidden

Task 2: Imagine you are a metro employee. A foreign passenger with a durian in her suitcase is not willing to go through the security check. Fill in the blanks according to the Chinese version provided in the brackets. Then act the dialogue out with your partner.

1. Would you please put your suitcase on the belt and go through the security check
2. ensure your safety
3. has the duty to go through the security check
4. What should I do
5. Would you please open your suitcase
6. According to the regulations
7. throw it away or take other means of transportation
8. Thank you for your cooperation.

Task 4: Translate the following sentences into English.

1. Security check is to ensure the safety of all passengers on the subway.
2. The security check only takes a minute or two. Passengers just need to put their bags or suitcases on the belt of the X-ray scanner.
3. The subway / metro stations are not responsible for keeping passengers' personal belongings.
4. It is prohibited to take the train with dangerous objects that are easy to explode or burn.
5. According to the regulations, anything smelly is banned on subway.
6. Balloons may explode on the subway, leading to a panic or a stampede.

Lesson 8 Security Warnings in the Station

I. Warming-up

Task 1: Work in pairs and match the English words or phrases with their corresponding Chinese meanings.

1~5: caebd

III. Exercises

Task 1: **Fill in the blanks with the words given in the box. Change the form if necessary.**

1. Put out
2. escalator
3. seal
4. luggage
5. circumstances
6. chasing

Task 2: **Imagine you are a metro employee. An elder foreign passenger carrying over size luggage is going to use the escalator. Persuade him to use a lift instead and help him with his luggage. Fill in the blanks according to the Chinese version provided in the brackets. Then act the dialogue out with your partner.**

1. For your safety
2. Where is the lift
3. Can I help you with your luggage
4. press the lift emergency stop button
5. could only be pressed under emergency
6. Please wait for a moment

Task 4: **Translate the following sentences into English.**

1. Do not chase others or engage in game-fight with each other in the station.
2. Please hold the handrail firmly and stand steadily at the right side of the escalator when riding/taking the escalator.
3. It is prohibited to touch the firefight equipment in the station without permission.
4. You should not have done that. The Escalator Emergency Stop Button could only be pressed under emergency.
5. Please do not destroy the equipment in the station.
6. Smoking is not allowed in the station.

Lesson 9 Security Warnings on the Platform

I. Warming-up

Task 1: **Look at the following pictures of the subway platforms in different cities. Discuss them with your partner and try to guess the names of the cities.**

1. Hangzhou
2. Beijing
3. Hong Kong
4. Shanghai

III. Exercises

Task 1: Fill in the blanks with the words given in the box. Change the form if necessary.

1. pressure
2. damage
3. moreover
4. attempt to
5. relieve
6. photographing
7. picked up
8. additional

Task 2: Imagine you are a metro employee. There are two kids playing and running near the tracks. Fill in the blanks according to the Chinese version provided in the brackets. Then act the dialogue out with your partner.

1. it is very dangerous to play or run near the tracks
2. Sorry. I didn't know.
3. fall onto the tracks
4. Thank you for your warning!
5. Would you please help me to pick it up?
6. stops operating
7. That's what we should do.

Task 4: Translate the following sentences into English.

1. Please do not take photos in the station.
2. Please stand behind the yellow safety line.
3. This is the final stop. Please transfer at the opposite if you want to continue traveling.
4. Please don't play or run in the station.
5. Please take care of your children.
6. Please mind the gap between the train and the platform.

Unit 4　Customer Service in Special Situations

Lesson 10　Helping the Sick, the Injured and the Disabled

I. Warming-up

Task 1: Work in pairs to match the words and phrases in the box with the following pictures.

1~6: BAFDEC

III. Exercises

Task 1: Fill in the blanks with the words or phrases given in the box. Change the form if necessary.

1. sponge
2. malfunction
3. dizzy
4. at your service
5. to relieve
6. were trapped
7. scene
8. attach importance to

Task 2: Fill in the blanks according to the Chinese given in the brackets. Then act the dialogue out with your partner.

1. Sir, are you all right?
2. Do you bring the medicine with you?
3. I'm out of breath
4. I will bring the medicine for you right away
5. Do I need to inform your family?
6. I feel much better after taking the medicine.
7. I was injured by the door
8. My arms can't move
9. We'll call an ambulance for you at once
10. accompany you to the hospital.

Task 4: Translate the following sentences into English.

1. The first aid personnel should take the heat-stroke passenger to an air-conditioned room and sponge him down with cold water.
2. Sorry, my friend is not feeling well, he has a heart attack. Could you help to call an ambulance?
3. I'll be fine after having a rest.
4. Excuse me, how can I enter the station and get on the train in the wheelchair?
5. I have an intense pain in my left wrist. Maybe I have my left wrist broken.

Lesson 11 Lost and Found

I. Warming-up

Task 1: Work in pairs to match the words and phrases in the box with the following pictures.

1~5: GBFCD   6~8: AEH

III. Exercises

Task 1: Fill in the blanks with the words or phrases given in the box. Change the form if necessary.

1. fill out
2. relevant
3. exactly
4. The moment
5. turn in
6. diploma
7. was bound for
8. pull out of
9. is claimed
10. appearance

Task 2: Fill in the blanks according to the Chinese given in the brackets. Then act the dialogue out with your partner.

1. I just dropped my iPhone into the tracks
2. in a plastic transparent protective cover
3. leave your phone number and get it in an appointed time.
4. We will retrieve your iPhone at the train interval
5. uses a third rail as power
6. only after the end of operation
7. I am eager to go to work
8. the arrival time and direction of the train
9. can you describe your umbrella?
10. I will contact you as soon as we find it.

Task 4: Translate the following sentences into English.

1. I left my umbrella on the train. What should I do?
2. We can't pick up your mobile phone while the trains are running. Please leave me your phone number so we can contact you later.
3. Please tell me the time and direction of the train
4. Would you tell me your name and phone number? I will contact you as soon as we find it.
5. Oh, my god! My mobile phone fell from the platform.

Lesson 12 Dealing with Emergency

I. Warming-up

Task 1: Work in pairs to translate the following words and phrases about subway devices or some causes of subway breakdowns into Chinese.

1. 火灾报警器

2. 紧急出口
3. 通话机
4. 紧急锤
5. 紧急停车按钮
6. 紧急解锁装置
7. 紧急门把手
8. 灭火器
9. 紧急求助电话
10. 消防电话插孔
11. 紧急刹车
12. 信号故障
13. 停电
14. 刹车故障
15. 自动扶梯故障

III. Exercises

Task 1:Fill in the blanks with the words or phrases given in the box. Change the form if necessary.

1. was transferred
2. scared
3. in order
4. reset
5. In case of
6. dragged
7. subconscious
8. appropriate
9. were evacuated
10. rescued

Task 2:Fill in the blanks according to the Chinese given in the brackets. Then act the dialogue out with your partner.

1. needs to be adjusted for some reasons
2. follow the instructions
3. pay attention to the station's broadcasting
4. refund the ticket
5. on your next ride
6. The platform is on fire
7. there is a lot of dense smoke
8. Please go to the concourse right away
9. evacuate passengers outside the station

10. exit the station immediately

Task 4: Translate the following sentences into English.

1. Attention please! Due to an emergency, we must evacuate the train.
2. Don't panic. Please follow the instructions of the platform attendant to leave the station as soon as possible.
3. You can return the ticket to the ticket office.
4. What's up? Why is there so much dense smoke?
5. Please move to the middle of the platform and get out of the station according to the evacuation signs.

Lesson 13 Operating in Adverse Weather

I. Warming-up

Task 1: Work in pairs to write out the English words or phrases about adverse climate according to given Chinese.

1. rainstorm
2. snowstorm
3. heavy rain
4. dust storm / sand storm
5. heavy snow
6. heavy fog
7. hurricane
8. typhoon
9. hail
10. thunderstorm
11. lightning
12. freezing

III. Exercises

Task 1: Fill in the blanks with the words or phrases given in the box. Change the form if necessary.

1. was distributed
2. in service
3. passage
4. out of service
5. mat
6. disposable

Task 2: Fill in the blanks according to the Chinese given in the brackets. Then act the dialogue out with your partner.

1. mind your step

2. wet and slippery

3. In order to keep the order of the station

4. don't crowd / stay at the exit

5. if there is a convenient umbrella

Task 4: Translate the following sentences into English.

1. Please take care when walking, the floor is wet and slippery.

2. Do you need some water and cooling ointment? It will relieve your symptom.

3. Metro trains are out of service due to the typhoon.

4. We will try our best to ensure the normal operation of the train in the heavy rain.

Unit 5　Customer Service for Big Events

Lesson 14　Greetings and Inquiring

I. Warming-up

Task 1: Work in pairs. Match the following logos with the correct event names.

1~6: debfac

III. Exercises

Task 1: Fill in the blanks with the words given in the box. Change the form if necessary.

1. legend

2. transportation

3. It is said to be

4. be impressed by

5. wetland

6. traffic

Task 2: Imagine you are a metro employee. You meet a foreign visitor at the metro station. Fill in the blanks according to the Chinese version provided in the brackets. Then act the dialogue out with your partner.

1. Could you do me a favor? / Can you help me?

2. I'm a member of the metro staff here.

3. Do you know where I can find a hotel?

4. I prefer a luxury one.

5. You can see the hotel when you get out of the metro station.

6. Have a nice trip.

Task 4: Translate the following sentences into English.

1. Welcome to Hangzhou. I'm glad to meet you.

2. I'm looking for the washroom. Can you show me where it is?

3. Of course. Actually, the nearest one is over there.

4. It is very convenient to take subway/metro.

5. Wish you have a safe trip.

6. You can take Line 1 to East Railway Station.

Lesson 15　The First and Last Train

I. Warming-up

Task 1：Match the following times with their corresponding English translations.

1~5：bdeca

III. Exercises

Task 1：Fill in the blanks with the words given in the box. Change the form if necessary.

1. wonder

2. will depart / departs / departed

3. intervals

4. time change

5. the last train

6. notice

Task 2：Imagine you are a metro employee. You meet a foreign passenger at the metro station. Fill in the blanks according to the Chinese version provided in the brackets. Then act the dialogue out with your partner.

1. Sure. What's wrong?

2. What should I do?

3. Let me check it for you.

4. You can take Line 4 to Xidan Station.

5. I don't think I can catch up with the train.

6. Have a safe trip.

Task 4：Translate the following sentences into English.

1. When is the first train?

2. How long should I wait then?

3. Last one just passed.

4. It's rush hour. The train arrives every 3 minutes, thus, you don't need to wait for a long time.

5. I think I might have missed the last train of Line 2.

6. I wonder if there is a time change for the last train at this station during the G20.

Lesson 16　Public Service

I. Warming-up

Task 1：Match the English words or phrases with their corresponding pictures.

1~4：dacb

III. Exercises

Task 1: Fill in the blanks with the words given in the box. Change the form if necessary.

1. twisted
2. deposit
3. lounge
4. inconvenience
5. accidental
6. be out of

Task 2: Imagine you are a metro employee. A foreign passenger is asking for a metro map. Fill in the blanks according to the Chinese version provided in the brackets. Then act the dialogue out with your partner.

1. May I ask you a question?
2. Go ahead, please.
3. I wonder where I can get a metro map.
4. Can I have a metro map?
5. We have just handed out all the maps here.
6. Or you can have one at other stations.

Task 4: Translate the following sentences into English.

1. Let me take you there.
2. We'll go through the special passage.
3. Sorry, There is no wheelchair-accessible toilet available in our station. You can go to Longxiangqiao Station.
4. For security reasons, you can't deposit luggage in a metro station during the Asian Games.
5. I'll show you the way on the map.
6. All metro stations in Shanghai are wheelchair-accessible.

Lesson 17　The Asian Games

I. Warming-up

Task 1: Work in pairs. Match the following scenic spots with their names.

1~6: dcafbe

III. Exercises

Task 1: Fill in the blanks with the words given in the box. Change the form if necessary.

1. upgrade
2. paradise
3. typical
4. splendid

5. through ages
6. heavens
7. heartfelt

Task 2: Imagine you are a metro employee, and you are introducing the local famous food to a foreign passenger. Fill in the blanks according to the Chinese version provided in the brackets. Then act the dialogue out with your partner.

1. I'm new here.
2. What can I do for you?
3. It's my first time here.
4. Would you please give me some advice?
5. Sounds great.
6. You may have a look there.
7. How can I get there?
8. You can take Line 1 and get off at Hubin Station.

Task 4: Translate the following sentences into English.

1. Hangzhou is a world-famous tourist city.
2. The main venue of Hangzhou Asian Games is located at Hangzhou Olympic and International Expo Center.
3. The metro will work over night on the day of the Opening Ceremony.
4. The subway security check will be upgraded during the Asian Games.
5. During the Asian Games, the metro departing interval is 3 minutes.

Appendix 7
References 参考文献

［1］程逆．城市轨道交通客运服务英语口语［M］．北京：人民交通出版社股份有限公司，2017．

［2］程钢．城市轨道交通专业英语（运营管理方向）［M］．北京：电子工业出版社，2017．

［3］赵巍巍．城市轨道交通客运服务英语（第2版）［M］．北京：人民交通出版社，2011．

［4］杨国平．城市轨道交通实用英语［M］．北京：外语教学与研究出版社，2012．

［5］刘聪慧，贾文婷．城市轨道交通专业英语［M］．北京：北京交通大学出版社，2015．

［6］颜景林．城轨交通客服英语口语100例［M］．北京：科学出版社，2015．